D1558670

ACTING AND THINKING:
THE POLITICAL THOUGHT
OF HANNAH ARENDT

ACTING AND THINKING

THE POLITICAL THOUGHT OF HANNAH ARENDT

LEAH BRADSHAW

UNIVERSITY OF TORONTO PRESS

Toronto Buffalo London

© University of Toronto Press 1989
Toronto Buffalo London
Printed in Canada

ISBN 0-8020-2625-7

Printed on acid-free paper

Canadian Cataloguing in Publication Data

Bradshaw, Leah, 1954–
Acting and thinking

Bibliography: p.
Includes index.
ISBN 0-8020-2625-7

1. Arendt, Hannah. 2. Political science –
Philosophy. I. Title.

JC251.A74B73 1989   320.5'092'4   C88-095388-8

This book has been published with the help of a grant from
the Canadian Federation for the Humanities, using funds provided by
the Social Sciences and Humanities Research Council of Canada.

For
Geoffrey Hamilton Bradshaw
and
Emma Catherine Planinc

Contents

Acknowledgments

Hannah Arendt once said that she really believed that 'you can only act in concert' and 'you can only think by yourself.' Yet she knew well that the solitariness of thinking is relieved, and provoked, by conversations with others. In reflecting upon Arendt's work, I have been fortunate to have the friendship of Zdravko Planinc, Barry Cooper, and Christian Lenhardt. I would like to thank them, and to express my particular debt to Christian Lenhardt, who gave counsel and direction to my studies.

There are others who had less to do specifically with the generation of thoughts here, but from whom I have learned much about politics and philosophy over many years. They are David Bedford, Tom Darby, Claudio Katz, William Shearson, and Gerald Etienne Tucker. Finally, I am grateful to R.I.K. Davidson and John St James of the University of Toronto Press for their helpful suggestions.

ACTING AND THINKING:
THE POLITICAL THOUGHT
OF HANNAH ARENDT

Introduction

This work investigates the ideas of one thinker, Hannah Arendt. To that extent, it is exegetical. In another sense, however, it is an inquiry into the activity of theorizing about politics in general, that is, into the relation between theory and the practice of politics. Arendt is an appropriate vehicle for this inquiry because the investigation of the theory/practice relation is the dominant theme in her writings. When I began this study, I was captivated by Arendt's powerful defence of political action in *The Human Condition* and thought that she had provided an original understanding of the primacy of action over theory. I did not initially have a comprehensive understanding of her work, nor had I unravelled all the complex arguments of *The Human Condition*. To me, the attraction of Arendt was really an impressionistic one. I was drawn to her choice of topics, her unnerving style, and her bravado in sweeping aside many of the conventional assumptions of the tradition of political theory.

In a single sentence, the central thesis of *The Human Condition* can be summarized as follows: action and speech are the supreme expressions of civilization, for they reveal plurality and freedom as constitutive elements of a distinctly human existence.[1] Contrary to much of the Western tradition, Arendt celebrated action, along with contemplation, as a quintessential human activity. 'A life without speech and action,' she wrote, 'is literally dead to the world.'[2] She proposed to look at the realm of action and speech – a realm that she often characterized as coextensive with the public or political realm – without bringing to it the intellectualist prejudices of theory.[3] She wanted to see what this realm would yield of its own accord and, indeed, she discovered some surprising things there.

Arendt's approach to the study of politics, and particularly her refusal to measure the worth of the political realm by the standards of the *vita contemplativa*, seemed a possible way out of what I perceived to be an impasse in political theory;

this impasse I would describe roughly as the contest between the ancient and the modern modes of theoretical inquiry. Though these two modes are quite different, they share a common disdain for the inherent freedom of political activity. I will explain what I mean briefly, since this sweeping critique of the tradition of political thought is Arendt's starting-point.

In the ancients' depiction of political life, all other accounts have been dwarfed by the formative contributions of Plato and Aristotle. In both these theorists we find a conception of politics and the realm of action that is situated in the context of a commitment to a transcendent view of justice. The city of Plato's *Republic* is an image in speech of the innate structure of the soul. Plato gives an account of the difference between opinion and truth, the object of politics and the object of contemplation, that has indelibly put its mark on all subsequent theorizing. He argues against his interlocutors that justice and virtue, the greatest of all goods, are not subject to the transience of the political world. The just man is a man who lives among others, but his justness does not derive from his participation in the plurality; it derives from his contemplative disposition. The argument of the *Republic* concludes that the life of the philosopher, the most virtuous of all lives, is incompatible with the life of the *polis*. Though virtue and justice are best understood by the philosopher, there is no indication in the *Republic* that the political realm could ever approximate this virtue and justice, nor is there any compelling reason why the philosopher ought to engage in political activity since his 'good' is not derived from, or dependent on, the shared public realm. Aristotle is often regarded as having praised the dignity of politics, but though there is a much closer attention paid in his work to the particular manifestations, traditions, and habits of political communities, the worth of political things is ultimately diminished by his statement in the *Nichomachean Ethics* that the man of intellectual virtue is the best man because he is the most self-sufficient.

The ancients' view of the contemplative life as a solitary, quiet pursuit contrasting with the noisy diversity of the active life remains the definitive account of the human condition until the modern period. Christian thought introduced new insights into the meaning of historical change, and reformulated the object of contemplation so as to combine thought with faith, but the basic dichotomy between the plural, political realm and the transcendent object of ascetic veneration remains constant. 'The moderns' make their entrance with Hegel and Marx who are the first to break with this dualism between thought and action. Hegel and Marx seem to have altered fundamentally this hierarchy of thought and action by elevating history to a new stature. Both begin with the notion that man as a being is constituted in time, and both regard contemplation as the consideration of man's genesis in history rather than as the dwelling upon a transcendent truth. This would appear to be an overcoming of the dualism between thought and action since a common object (history) is the locus of both activities. In fact, the dualism is not overcome; it is merely submerged.

The truth claims of Hegel and Marx depend upon whether they can prove that history somehow 'progresses.' Looking back at history in its linear course, both see a logic that appears in hindsight to have been immanent in human affairs. The chain of necessity that Hegel and Marx discover in history subverts the possibility that *freedom* of action is the catalyst of progress. All action in retrospect appears to have been necessary, not free. Moreover, in claiming that it is possible from a modern standpoint to grasp the nature of historical change in its cumulative entirety, Hegel and Marx claim to have complete knowledge of the human condition. Both contend, in addition, that in the post-historical context human beings will be rational and free subjects. Implied in their theoretical understanding is the idea that unpredictability, creativity, and innovation are eradicated from politics. The Hegelian-Marxist account of the relationship between thought and action may be very different from the Platonic-Aristotelian one, in that it eliminates the dualism between transcendent truth and historical contingency, but the consequences for action are similar. The result is a theoretical 'clamp' upon action.[4]

This polarization between ancient and modern modes of theory is exaggerated, I realize, but it does seem that much of contemporary political theory rests on one side or the other of this spectrum. One of the most dominant trends in political theory in North America stems from the writings of Leo Strauss and his followers, who defend the Platonic-Aristotelian notion of virtue against what they perceive to be the misguided direction of modern historicism. Eric Voegelin has pursued a similar course, referring to all modern theory as symptomatic of the gnostic syndrome. From the modern standpoint, there are many post-Marxist revisionists who are attempting to amend the basic principles of Marx's theory in order to accommodate it to a rapidly changing world. In general, the notion first conceived by Hegel and Marx – that history generates meaning, and that that meaning subsequently becomes a pattern by which action is understood – has become an accepted method of procedure in the social sciences. The preoccupation with classifying phenomena, prediction, and 'model-building' is a consequence of the modern idea that action can be rationalized by the imposition of theory. In short, there is a tendency in modern theory to repress the revelatory capacity of the phenomena and to seek instead to manipulate it through the imposition of preconceived theoretical conceptions.

Hannah Arendt represents a radical departure from the positions outlined so far. In essence, she rejected the assumptions of both the ancient and modern modes of theorizing. She resisted the idea that there is a transcendent object of contemplation from which affairs of the world are judged and the idea that history generates some comprehensive meaning 'acting behind the backs of men.' She offered an account of the political realm that deliberately counterposed itself to the *vita contemplativa* and that stood 'in manifest contradiction to the tradition.'[5] Beginning from such a position, Arendt attempted to eliminate the tyranny of theory over action and to recover the integrity of the *vita activa*.

This book begins with an exploratory analysis of *The Human Condition*, where Arendt sets out her defence of political action. Published in 1958, *The Human Condition* was the first of Arendt's two major philosophical works. The second work of this sort, *The Life of the Mind*, was her last. Between these two lies a time span of over twenty-five years during which Arendt garnered a controversial reputation for many things: her thoughts on revolution, on Zionism, on integration in the southern United States, and most important, her reflections on the trial of Nazi war criminal Adolf Eichmann. She was a prolific writer and somewhat of a popular one, contributing frequently to New York publications like the *Partisan Review*, *Commmentary*, and the *New Yorker*. Her reputation as an astute, if unconventional critic of contemporary politics was established before the release of *The Human Condition*, with her publication in the early fifties of *The Origins of Totalitarianism*. Though Arendt is remembered best, it seems, for her commentaries on political events in the twentieth century, her two great contributions to political theory are *The Human Condition* and *The Life of the Mind*. These works address themselves explicitly to ontological concerns. Yet there is a major difference between the two that can be understood only by piecing together the experiences and ideas that filled the quarter of a century between them. *The Life of the Mind* is about thinking, not acting, and it treats thinking as a separate, autonomous dimension of human existence.

The organization of this book is logical rather than chronological. It moves from *The Human Condition* to *The Life of the Mind*, treating these two works as the border marks that define the full range of Arendt's thought. Chronologically, there are publications that appeared before *The Human Condition*, but none of these earlier works contains a systematic reflection on the relationship of thought to action. *The Human Condition* is a carefully thought out statement in defence of the *vita activa* whose categories and concepts appear in embryonic form in some of the earlier essays and in the study of totalitarianism. In chapter 1, I look at *The Human Condition* and the critical responses to it, comparing the ideas in that work to some earlier essays. From this inquiry, it becomes evident that Arendt had serious problems trying to explicate the *vita activa* without discussing the role of thinking.

The second chapter analyses Arendt's more political works, including her study of totalitarianism and her various writings on revolution and society. Her commentaries on political movements in the twentieth century show that while she maintained her emphasis upon plurality, action, and freedom as the supreme expressions of the human condition, she simultaneously indicated the practical impossibility of achieving these ideals. Despite the difficulties and contradictions encountered in defending the primacy of action, Arendt continued to hold this view until she reported on the trial of Adolf Eichmann. This was the turning-point in her thinking.

Chapter 3 looks at Arendt's recounting of the trial and at the passionate responses it evoked from critics, and explains the connection between her reflections on Eichmann and her reformulation of the relationship between action and thought. Eichmann's 'banality' appeared to Arendt to have been the result of his inability, or unwillingness, to think. His crime consisted in the fact that he simply drifted with the tide of political change in the Germany of the 1930s, never pausing to think critically about his own actions. Arendt was convinced by the example of Eichmann that thinking autonomously – that is, detaching oneself from the world of appearances – was absolutely essential for acting morally. By arguing that Eichmann could have acted differently than he did, Arendt was thrown back upon the antithesis between thinking and acting. Eichmann should have been able to make independent judgments, but this requires that one has the capacity to think outside the formative context of the plural, political realm.

How can we sustain the position that the human condition is formed in the context of plurality, interdependence, and shared opinions, and at the same time demand that human beings be able to *judge* that realm? This is the question that Arendt pursued painstakingly in *The Life of the Mind*. Chapter 4 is devoted entirely to the schematic of this last work. In it, Arendt tried to substantiate the autonomy of thought without thereby reverting to the metaphysical dualism between appearance and truth, and without subordinating the political realm to the abstract imperatives of thought. Her breakdown of the processes of 'mental life' into the three faculties of thinking, willing, and judging is, I found, a profound and eloquent way of expressing the fundamental unity of thought and world, while still providing for the reflective distance that is the prerequisite of all critical thinking. *The Life of the Mind* is an attempt to integrate thought and action as the constituent elements of the human condition. In the final chapter, I consider the implications of this work for political actors.

As these general introductory comments indicate, I did not find that Arendt's work as a whole was able to bear the promise of *The Human Condition*. *The Life of the Mind* repudiates the basic assumption of that book: that the *vita activa* can stand on its own, without interference from or judgment by the *vita contemplativa*. When Arendt came belatedly to her reconsideration of the importance of thinking for political action, she was obliged to resurrect all the old 'metaphysical dogmas,' as she termed them, and to examine them with new interest. She found that the theoretical prejudice towards the solitary life of contemplation and the tendency among philosophers to search for ways to control freedom of action were born out of a legitimate existential dilemma.[6] Arendt never relinquished her admiration for the political actor, or abandoned her delight in the unpredictability of political life, but she acquired an equal admiration for the solitary thinker whose path runs often parallel to that of the political actor without ever converging with it.

Though Arendt was unable to make action immune to judgment by the standards of thought, it became clear to me in writing this work that this is not a personal failing of Arendt's, but rather a task that is rendered impossible by the very nature of reflection. The space between action and thought, and the withdrawal and judgmental nature of thinking, are necessary pre-conditions for responsible action. Arendt's resoluteness in defending action was not without consequence, however. Because of her commitment to the revelatory capacity of the world of appearances, she was able to provide an account of the relationship between thinking and acting that avoids both the dualism between politics and the search for truth, and the subsumption of thinking and acting under the progressivist conception of history that is so dominant among modern political thinkers. Arendt manages to conceptualize thinking in such a way as to preserve the integral worth of political freedom. She does this by evoking for us the ground that unites the thinking and acting being. This, as I shall try to elucidate, is Hannah Arendt's achievement.

1 In Defence of Action

The Vita Activa *and* The Human Condition

In the prologue to *The Human Condition*, Arendt explained to the reader why she had chosen to write a book with such a formidable title. She wrote that the inquiry had been prompted by her own fear that modern man may be 'possessed by a rebellion against human existence as it has been given.'[1] She feared that Western civilization had altered something in man but she was reluctant to call it human nature; she thought that the substance of man's nature was beyond the comprehension of human beings who are born into a cosmic order that they did not create and cannot control. All Arendt was willing to say was that insofar as man is a political being – that is, a living, speaking, and acting creature – he can find his existence meaningful only if his understanding of the world is shared by others. This shared meaning, for her, was the human condition and she was concerned that this web of meaning was no longer secure.

Arendt was explicit about the distinction between human *nature* and the human *condition*. She wrote: 'To avoid misunderstanding: the human condition is not the same as human nature, and the sum total of human activities and capabilities which correspond to the human condition does not constitute anything like human nature.'[2] We cannot speak meaningfully about human nature, said Arendt, because human beings did not create themselves and therefore do not have access to a complete knowledge of their own being. They are born into a world that antecedes them: 'If we have a nature or essence, then surely only a god could know and define it.' In contrast, the human condition, according to her, is knowable and definable because it consists of the capacities and characteristics that human beings have cultivated together to create a truly humanized existence: 'Whatever enters the human world of its own accord or is drawn into it by human effort becomes part of the human condition. The impact of the world's reality upon human existence is felt and received as a conditioning force.'[3]

In other words, the human condition, in contrast to 'human nature,' is not something that seeks to define itself according to a static essence. It is the sum total of human activities that generate a peculiarly human environment. History, consequently, is an integral part of the human condition. History, in fact, is the concrete proof of man's capacity to build a world. Its creation can be attributed to certain discernible capacities, of which Arendt emphasized those of labour, work, and action. Thinking is also an integral part of the human condition, but Arendt chose to exclude thinking from her considerations, and chose instead to concentrate upon what she termed the *vita activa*, whose exclusive components consist of labour, work, and action. Her reasons for excluding thinking, and the problems encountered because of this omission, will become apparent in the discussion of this chapter.

In Arendt's formulation, the three capacities of labour, work, and action constitute the *vita activa*: a realm of 'human life insofar as it is actively engaged in doing something,' Each capacity corresponds to a particular aspect of human existence: labour corresponds to the production and reproduction of the means of survival; work to artifice and home-building; and action to the condition of human plurality. In sum, man is a biological animal, a builder, and a participant in community. To the extent that he has to provide for his own sustenance, man is bound to labour, essentially a repetitious but necessary form of activity. But human beings also want to create a world that is distinctly human and beautiful. The home that they create in the world exhibits an ingenuity that far surpasses the means required to sustain life. It exhibits the capacity for work. Action, the third of man's capacities, and the foundation of political life, is related neither to brute survival nor to the provision of a world of useful and beautiful objects. It is the one capacity that depends upon shared experience and communication, and the one sphere of activity that demonstrates both sameness and difference among human beings. Action is the highest expression of the human condition, we might conjecture, because it is a kind of synthetic embodiment of our commonality as natural (labouring) creatures and our distinctiveness as creative (working) individuals. Since labour enacts only the quality of sameness (everyone eats and produces), and work only difference (each man crafts a tool or creates a work of art in accordance with his specific desires and his perception of beauty), neither of these forms of activity can fully express what it is to be a human being.

Action is the most important part of the *vita activa* but it is also the most obscure of Arendt's categories. She tells us that action is history. It is men acting in the plural, creating and destroying communities and performing other sorts of changes in the world that subsequently are recorded by historians and story-tellers. History tells the story of unique events, yet history in this sense is possible only because of the continual regeneration of the species. For Arendt, natality was the motor behind action and politics. This, as she noted, contrasts sharply with the classical Greek notion that philosophy is equivalent to dying.

> The philosopher's experience of the eternal, which to Plato was *arrhēton* ('unspeakable') and to Aristotle *aneu logou* ('without word') and which later was conceptualized in the paradoxical *nunc stans* ('the standing now'), can occur only outside the realm of human affairs and outside the plurality of men, as we know from the Cave parable in Plato's *Republic*, where the philosopher, having liberated himself from the fetters that bound him to his fellow men, leaves the cave in perfect 'singularity,' as it were, neither accompanied nor followed by others. Politically speaking, if to die is the same thing as 'to cease to be among men,' experience of the eternal is a kind of death and the only thing that separates it from real death is that it is not final because no living creature can endure it for any length of time.[4]

Each individual, considering the nature of his soul and its destination, may have to come to terms with his own individual death, but communities of men are concerned with the durability of the polity and the continuity of the species that transcends the death of any one of its individual members.

Arendt thought that the concerns of the philosopher and those of the political actor were necessarily different, and she dated the separation of the two from the time of ancient Greece. According to her account, it was Plato who first distiguished the realm of contemplation from that of politics, according the activity of thinking a higher status than that of political action.[5] This hierarchy was based on the knowledge that no work of human hands could approximate the creation of the cosmos, whose origins remain a mystery and, accordingly, that man's highest activity ought to be the contemplation of things divine. What Arendt objected to was this hierarchy. Ever since Plato men have considered the *vita activa* inferior to the *vita contemplativa*; this emphasis has meant death to the political realm in several senses. Since philosophy dwelled on things divine, but since the divine mystery of life is death, the philosophers' preoccupation with dying has worked against the concerns of history, politics, action, and community, all of which are connected to man's birth and earthly immortality.

The ancient Greek philosophers distorted the importance of the *vita activa* by subordinating it to the aims of contemplation, but they recognized that political activity occupies an autonomous, meaningful, space in human affairs. Most significant for Arendt was the distinction they drew between public and private life. The activities of the household were regarded as pre-political, characterized by labour, authoritarianism, and, perhaps, violence. The private sanctuary of the household provided a space in which men could attend to all the necessities of life, namely reproduction, home-building, and education. Arendt wrote that all Greek philosophers maintained the radical separation of the private realm from the public, political realm: 'What all Greek philosophers ... took for granted is that freedom is exclusively located in the political realm, that necessity is primarily a prepolitical phenomenon, characteristic of the private household organization, and that force and violence are justified in this sphere because they are the only means to master necessity.'[6]

Arendt thought that this distinction between private and public realms had dissolved in the modern world, to the detriment of both. Politics has not suffered a loss of dignity at the hands of twentieth-century philosophers so much as from the attentions of social theorists whose prescriptions for politics usually entail some project for equalizing the economic and social status of all citizens. The result has been that governments are preoccupied with what Arendt called 'housekeeping duties.'

We should pause here to clarify what Arendt meant by 'society' and the 'social question,' since she used these terms to describe a modern phenomenon that she counterposed to the ancient dichotomy between private and public realms. Whereas, according to the ancient Greek account, the private realm was that in which the necessities of life were attended to and the public realm was that in which necessity was left behind in order to pursue freedom as an end in itself, in the modern context the distinction between these two spheres of activity has been blurred by what Arendt called the intervening category of 'society.' Society seemed to denote for Arendt two predominant characteristics. On the one hand, she described it as the elevation of the concerns of the private realm into the public domain. Society emerges when the activities of the household become matters of public concern: 'The emergence of society – the rise of housekeeping, its activities, problems, and organizational devices – from the shadowy interior of the household into the light of the public sphere, has not only blurred the old borderline between private and political, it has also changed almost beyond recognition the meaning of the two terms and the significance for the life of the individual and the citizen.'[7] However, society is not simply the encroachment of formerly private matters into the public realm. It also signified for Arendt a public arena in which human beings are assigned a common identity or a common characteristic. Citizens are replaced by functionaries, and politics becomes servant to the preservation of society, whether that society be 'a society of the faithful as in the Middle Ages, or a society of property-owners as in Locke, or a society relentlessly engaged in a process of acquisition, as in Hobbes, or a society of producers as in Marx, or a society of jobholders as in our own society.'[8] What all these descriptions of 'societies' have in common is that in all of them, according to

Arendt, the freedom of the political realm was forfeited in making politics subservient to a dominant interest. Society tyrannizes over politics. Arendt thought that the modern 'society of jobholders' was particularly damaging to politics, however, because it is this most recent phenomenon that has made the most private of all activities (labour) the highest political principle.

If we look at what Arendt considered to be the two principal enemies of politics – philosophy and society – we can see that they are denounced by her because each emphasizes one feature of the human condition to the exclusion of others. Philosophy is antithetical to politics because it stresses the life and thought of the individual; society is antagonistic to politics since it is chiefly concerned with the common 'housekeeping' needs of men. The juxtaposition of political action to philosophizing and social housekeeping is similar to the contrast of action with work and labour. Philosophy is an enemy of politics because traditional philosophy, as Arendt understood it, was based on the model of work. And society is anathema to politics because it is occupied with the labouring activity. After her opening comments in *The Human Condition*, directed at the debilitating effects that philosophy and society have on politics, Arendt turned to what she thought was the real root of the problem in the Western tradition: the glorification of work in earlier polities and, worse, the emphasis on labour in modern ones. Just as she regarded labour as an activity inferior to work, and both of them as inferior to action, so too she regarded modern conceptions of politics as inferior to ancient ones, and both of them as inferior to what politics *could be*.

The criterion by which Arendt judged the quality of life in any era was stated quite clearly: 'Human life, insofar as it is world-building, is engaged in a constant process of reification, and the degree of worldliness of produced things, which all together form the human artifice, depends upon their greater or lesser permanence in the world itself.'[9] The permanence of things, in turn, depends upon two things: (1) the presence of others who will recognize and remember human achievements, and (2) the ability of human beings to objectify themselves in work. 'Worldliness,' then, is a judgment made by human beings about the world they have constituted. Accordingly, it is a judgment made of all that is not natural or given. The objects of work are our most immediate reminders of the worldly character of our lives, for in creating new objects man 'takes matter out of nature's hands without giving it back to her in the swift course of the natural metabolism of the living body.'[10]

In contrast to the activity of work, which destroys nature so that a human world might be created, labour is fully a part of the natural order. From the standpoint of worldliness, labour is the least desirable of all human activities, but from the standpoint of nature, it is the most 'blessed.' Arendt spoke reverently of labour as the 'sheer bliss' of being alive, a way of speaking that suggests that man could swing with nature's prescribed cycle. Such a blessing could never be encountered in work. But labour's blessedness does not make it any less futile. Arendt also called labour the 'darkness' of existence, or the pain of being alive. To pursue freedom from this pain was, for her, tantamount to seeking freedom from life itself. She wrote: 'The human condition is such that pain and effort are not just symptoms which can be removed without changing life itself; they are rather the modes in which life itself, together with the necessity to which it is bound, makes itself felt. For mortals, the "easy life of the gods" would be a lifeless cycle.'[11] Since labour is an irremediable 'given' condition of human existence, Arendt held that it was futile to think that any kind of political reform could alter the basic necessity or 'worldlessness' of this activity. She criticized Marx for making the labouring activity the basis of his theory of human emancipation. To think that labour could ever become the well-spring of a new consciousness was, for Arendt, to fundamentally misunderstand the limitations of it. 'Labor's products, the products of man's metabolism with nature, do not stay in the world long enough to become part of it, and the laboring activity itself, concentrated exclusively on life and its maintenance, is oblivious of the world to the point of worldlessness ... A mass society of laborers, such as Marx had in mind when he spoke of "socialized mankind," consists of worldless specimens of the species mankind.'[12]

Arendt portrayed modern Western democratic society as a society of labourers. In its display of consumerism and its disrespect for tradition and culture, it reflects the futility of *animal laborans*. Looking at the primary concerns of most modern men – acquisition, social welfare, and so on – Arendt concluded that they (or we) no longer know how to distinguish noble deeds from base ones, or beautiful objects from ugly ones. In the undifferentiated 'darkness' of society, all things are simply part of a natural process. Consequently, she commented that 'as long as the *animal laborans* remains in possession of it [the public realm] there can be no true public realm, but only private activities displayed in the open.'[13]

While *animal laborans* is a world-destroyer, *homo faber* is a world-builder. The products of work are different from those of labour in that they represent objectifications; they circumscribe an objective, and more or less permanent, man-made world. Unlike *animal laborans*, 'which is subject to the necessity of its own life,' and hence can only exist in a slavish dependence on the cycles of nature, *homo faber* is the 'master of himself and his doings.'[14] He is driven neither by necessity nor by the desire for public display, but pursues his activity for its own sake. The image evoked is one of the solitary craftsman who is satisfied by the pure utility or beauty of the objects he creates. The 'aloneness' of *homo faber* is in fact crucial to Arendt's analysis, for while it is true that the worker is the most independent of all men, depending on neither nature nor other men for the meaning of what he does, he is incapable of understanding how what he makes fits into a larger, interwoven network of fabricated things. *Homo faber* is the anchor of the human world, but is neither the necessary nor most meaningful condition for it. His solitariness is an illusion. His work-objects serve to ease the pain of labour, through the creation of tools, but they also secure the durability of action and speech through the writing of books, the erection of monuments, and so on. Without actions to record or labour to relieve, *homo faber* would be as 'worldless' as *animal laborans*. The meaning of work is ultimately derived from the human being as actor. For Arendt, a life without speech and action is 'dead to the world,' although certainly a life without labour would be literally dead. Here, then, we have an account of work that situates itself categorically between labour and action. Though work would be impossible without the foundation of labour and the need to provide for, and facilitate, basic sustenance, it is action that gives work its 'worldly' attributes by bestowing upon work-objects an aesthetic value that is not determined by necessity.

Even if work is meaningless without the world of action and speech, it has been the activity that predominated in most philosophical conceptions of man, up until the modern age. Arendt criticized ancient Greek philosophy in particular for trying to liberate *homo faber* from his dependence on the realm of action. Again, Plato committed the original error. Confronted with the frailty of human affairs, and the apparent haphazardness of political action, Plato attempted to establish the foundations of political order in such a way that order could be fabricated out of chaos.[15] The notion that political life is something that is made to accord with a specific end is drawn directly from the experience of work, according to Arendt. Just as the craftsman makes an object for a particular use, so too for Plato, the ideal political actor is the insightful ruler who moulds the *polis* for a particular end: the realization of justice. 'Plato, who was the first to design a blueprint for the making of political bodies, has remained the inspiration of all later utopias.'[16] Even though Arendt conceded that utopias have never played a prominent role in actual history, they have been the inspiration behind a tradition of political thought that has generally substituted making for acting. In ancient (Platonic and Aristotelian) thought, this meant that politics was interpreted according to philosophical models of truth; in medieval thought, it meant that politics was aimed at the salvation of souls; and in the modern context, it has meant that politics serves the interests of society.[17]

Any application of the model of work to politics denigrates action as a purposeful activity sui generis. For Plato, politics was not meaningful in itself, but only to the extent that it provided a secure space in which the philosopher could pursue his love of the divine. The Platonic philosopher's main concern was a solitary endeavour and the conditions of plurality that characterize political life could not help but impede his quiet contemplation. Likewise, for Augustine, Arendt's primary reference for medieval thought, 'the function of government is to enable the "good" to live more quietly among the "bad".'[18] Any polity, whether real or imagined, that denies the ability of men in concert to create meaning and turns instead to the notion that politics serves a higher end than itself is based on a fundamental misunderstanding of the three distinct aspects of the human condition.

Given that, according to Arendt's own account of the history of political thought, action has never been considered as the sole aim of political life, one wonders why she defended it so vociferously. She did so on the grounds that action has always been the most important activity of human existence even if it was not the motive of theory. Political theorists have avoided action as a category for serious thought because the very nature of action, its causes and outcomes, elude the theoretical attitude. Action is the 'sheer human togetherness' of human existence in which people disclose themselves to one another. Because human beings can reveal themselves fully only in this community of intersubjective meaning, the 'who' of a living, acting individual can never be revealed in words alone.[19] Arendt did not find this elusive understanding of action puzzling, nor did she think it surprising that the entire tradition of Western thought had failed (in her mind) to give an adequate account of human existence. She commented, in keeping with her original distinction between human nature and the human condition: it is a 'well-known philosophic impossibility to arrive at a definition of man.'[20]

The elusiveness of action is further compounded by the fact that the living person 'discloses himself' in a pluralistic web of meaning that itself changes and shifts from the impact of his own words and deeds. Consequently, though we can note changes in the constitution of human communities, we cannot point to the author, or authors of those changes, and we can never predict the outcome. 'The reason why each human life tells its story and why history ultimately becomes the storybook of mankind, with many actors and speakers and yet without any tangible authors, is that both are the outcome of action.'[21] The opaqueness of this force Arendt called action is what first led philosophers to neglect the realm of politics, the rise and fall of communities, as material for rigorous thought. Plato's image of the puppet-men being manipulated by some hidden force is a direct response to this inability to account for the origins of human action,[22] but Arendt claimed that one could see similar 'solutions' in the Christian conception of the invisible hand of God, the Hegelian construction of the mysterious force of world history, and other theoretical designs. All such formulations are derived from the inability to comprehend action, and all stand in defiance of a basic human understanding. 'The invisible actor behind the scenes is an invention arising from a mental perplexity but corresponding to no real experience.'[23]

If theory corresponds to no real experience (or, better, only to the experience of bewilderment), then what *is* the real experience of men? Arendt suggested that it was the common-sense acceptance of the revelatory capacity of speech and action.[24] Contrary to the philosopher, who is always searching for causes and predictable outcomes, the man of common sense has an innate trust in his own capabilities and limits. 'The human sense of reality demands that men actualize the sheer passive giveness of their being, not in order to change it but in order to make articulate and call into full existence what otherwise they would have to suffer passively anyhow.'[25] Arendt believed that men who had common sense could recognize in an intuitive way the 'gift' of speech and action, and could trust in their ability to live a meaningful existence, even though they could not give an account of it. Most men recognize courage, virtue, and justice when they see it in the acts and words of a living person, and this living recognition is always more complete, more wondrous, than the theoretical account. In all great men, Arendt wrote, the source of creativity 'springs indeed from *who* they are and remains outside the actual work process as well as independent of *what* they may achieve.'[26]

Unfortunately, even though common sense supposedly tells us of the importance of action, there has never been an age that mirrored the spirit of action in quite the way the modern world reflects the dominance of *animal laborans* or the ancient one reflected the aspirations of *homo faber*. Such an age would have to be one in which men had both a tremendous confidence in their own powers and also a respect for the necessary limits to rational understanding. The closest approximation that we have was the Greece depicted in Homeric epic; indeed Arendt wrote about this period often and with an almost nostalgic sentimentality. Short-lived though it was, Arendt exalted it as an age marked by the words and deeds of courageous men. Its death coincided, not surprisingly, with the first political philosophy.[27] For Arendt, it was as though once men began to think about the world they inhabited, they lost something of their capacities, or at least displaced these capacities on false objects and goals. With the advent of philosophy, action was deprived of its rightful expression in politics, and was deflected into other areas. Expelled from the political arena by philosopher-kings, tyrants, the forces of the market, and other odious forms of domination, action has been channelled into a perversion of its true form.

In the world dominated by *homo faber* man's capacity for action manifested itself in the exchange market. *Homo faber* does create some kind of public space for the disclosure of meaning in that he creates a forum for the exchange of products. Strictly speaking, this space of appearance is not a political one, since the market-place is intended to display products, not persons. Still, the objects of work and their exchange contribute to a tangible world, so the market-place meets at least one of Arendt's criteria of worldliness: reification. 'Workmanship,' she wrote, 'may be an unpolitical way of life but it certainly is not an anti-political one.'[28] Where the world of *homo faber* falls short of expressing all men's capacities is in its inability to create meaning. We recall that, for Arendt, he who crafts the objects that constitute an objective world does so only for utility and, sometimes, beauty; his activity must always be directed at some purposeful end that is outside the region of his technical understanding. But in a world that is empty of meaningful political action and community, the craft of *homo faber* loses its purpose. In such a world, 'worldliness' would then become confused with the making of things for their own sake, and human existence would be seen as an endless extension into the future where the production of one object is simply the means to produce another. Eventually, *homo faber* would cease to regard his activity as one of providing a stable, objective home for men in the world, and come to see it as a constant transformation of the world. As Arendt put it: 'The trouble with the utility standard inherent in the very activity of fabrication is that the relationship between means and ends on which it relies is very much like a chain whose every end can serve again as a means in some other context. In other words, in a strictly utilitarian world all ends are bound to be of short duration and to be transformed into means for some further ends.'[29]

It is a corruption of the activity of work to think of it as furnishing its own meaning, and this initial corruption leads to an even greater one. Once men start to view the products of their own hands as having no other end but to make more products, it is a short step from there to treating all the world, both natural and man-made, as the means to man's infinite making. 'Since it is in the nature of man the user and instrumentalizer to look upon everything as a means to an end – upon every tree as potential wood – this must eventually mean that man becomes the measure not only of things whose existence depends upon him but of literally everything there is.'[30] If one permits the standards of *homo faber* to rule the world he will 'eventually help himself to everything.'[31]

Once the leap is made from understanding the objective products of work as being for man's use to understanding all the world that way, we are in the realm of *animal laborans*. In Arendt's conceptual framework, there is an inevitable slide from one to the other. Since work is ultimately meaningless without the purpose of political action to sustain its worth, only the mute necessity of life remains to propel man onward. The mastery of *homo faber* degenerates into the slavishness of *animal laborans*; the objective world declines into the consumer world of modern society. For Arendt, this constitutes the lowest point in human history, at which the question of meaning does not make sense. 'Within the life process itself, of which laboring remains an integral part and which it never transcends, it is idle to ask questions that presuppose the category of means and ends, such as whether men live and consume in order to have strength to labour or whether they labor in order to have the means of consumption.'[32]

It is certainly a dismal picture that Arendt paints of the modern situation, although she did not think that modern man 'has lost his capacities or is on the point of losing them.'[33] What has happened is that, in a world dominated by *animal laborans*, meaningful activity 'escapes more and more the range of ordinary human experience,' which means that the 'space' of worldliness becomes increasingly smaller. Arendt stated that meaningful action in the modern world is restricted to artists and scientists, and even their activity is severely curtailed by the lack of a public space in which they can participate.[34]

The choice of artists and scientists as exclusive examples of men who have managed to escape the modern predicament is most peculiar. If we look more closely at the reasons Arendt gave for their resilience, it appears that these have nothing to do with any of the 'conditions' she described in *The Human Condition* as prerequisite for action. Art has survived as a meaningful activity because, though it is a form of work, it has a 'durability of a higher order' than other work-objects.[35] And science is a meaningful form of action because it depends on something more than a public space for acting and speaking; scientists have 'moral standards' and a 'code of honour' that have insulated them from the ill effects of modern society.[36] It turns out then that whatever remains of meaningful work and action in the modern world does not depend upon the conditions that Arendt herself had stipulated as necessary for their perpetuity. In spite of the fact that 'public space' has been destroyed and work denigrated by the all-pervasive influence of *animal laborans*, a few human beings have persisted in engaging in meaningful activity. Finally, we are told in the last paragraph of the book that the survival of the few in the midst of a devastated world might have something to do with the capacity for thought. The last paragraph ought to be cited here in full, for it effectively contradicts everything Arendt set out to do in *The Human Condition*: 'If no other test but the experience of being active, no other measure but the extent of sheer activity were to be applied to the various activities within the *vita activa*, it might well be that thinking as such would surpass them all. Whoever has any experience in this matter will know how right Cato was when he said: *Numquam se plus agere quam nihil cum ageret, numquam minus solum esse quam cum solus esset* – "Never is he more active than when he does nothing, never is he less alone than when he is by himself." '[37]

There is a double-barrelled problem posed by this intrusion of thought into the *vita activa*. First, Arendt had claimed that action was the expression of the 'sheer human togetherness' of human beings, that it had its origins in a common-sense understanding of the world, and that its importance could be recognized only within a network of human relations that holds intersubjective meaning in the highest esteem. Further, she had stated that while action thus defined was devalued by philosophy and 'social theory,' it survived in the real world. But, at the conclusion of her study we find that, indeed, action survives in the real world, not in the common-sense experience of the plurality of men, but in the isolated tasks of artistic creation and scientific thought. From this, we can conclude that action in the modern world is saved by the capacity that some human beings have for thought, which is something that Arendt had not considered at length in her work.

The second problem arises from the fact that Arendt's understanding of the gradual demise of the *vita activa*, from its glorious moment in Homeric Greece to its eventual decay in the modern world, can be traced back to changes in man's self-understanding. Thought has been both man's tool of destruction and his salvation. Earlier in the discussion, it was noted that for Arendt the first waning of the *vita activa* was coincidental with the inception of Western philosophy. Once man tried to grasp conceptually the meaning of action, he became exasperated with its apparent lack of cause or aim, and turned to images of divine mastery to explain the inexplicable. Arendt's chronicle of the history of Western civilization since that time described a necessary, logical path towards our present state of affairs. The history of Western civilization, however, is not the product of labourers and workers. The craftsman, working away in solitude on his 'tree,' is not responsible for a utilitarian world any more than the labourer, forced by necessity to eke out a living performing some menial task, is responsible for a consumer society. The changing character of worldliness is reflected in the changes in man's understanding of himself. *Homo faber* degenerated into *animal laborans* only when he began to view his tasks differently. Thought, not work or labour, is man's original sin in *The Human Condition*. It became truly dangerous once it was uncoupled from its object (the divine) and turned itself inward to the life-forces of man as a biological being.[38]

It was the thinkers of the modern age who made *animal laborans* the victor in the modern world. Just as Arendt pointed to Plato as the thinker who first gave the *vita activa* a bad name by subordinating it to the pursuit of the good, she pointed to what she called the modern 'life philosophers' – Nietzsche, Marx, and Bergson – as those thinkers who were responsible for equating Life with Being. For these modern life-philosophers, she said, 'their ultimate point of reference is not work and worldliness any more than action: it is life and life's fertility.'[39] And as we already know from Arendt's account of the three capacities that comprise the human condition, life and its fertility is the *one* capacity of man that is unworldly.

In conclusion, then, we have a mystifying problem. Arendt apparently excluded thought from among the activities that constitute the *vita activa*, but in fact thought was responsible for most of the miseries of Western civilization and at the same time it has preserved whatever is left of the *vita activa* in the twentieth century. The central critical question that emerges from *The Human Condition* then is: Why did Arendt categorically exclude thought from her analysis?

Most critical responses to *The Human Condition* raised this question, but few provided any real insight into a plausible answer. Reactions to the book immediately after its publication were diverse. Some critics praised it as a major breakthrough in political theory – one reviewer said it was 'the first important reevaluation of the human condition since Marx'[40] – and some castigated it for its moralizing tone. Another reviewer remarked that 'the pale light of a past golden age pervades the book, and there is little awareness of the grandeur and terror of the present.'[41] Margaret Canovan, author of the first book-length study of Hannah Arendt's thought, wrote that the main concern in *Human Condition* was with 'the various modes of human *activity* and their respective dignity': '[Arendt] is explicitly not concerned with trying to judge the relative merits of activity and thought.'[42] Yet Charles Frankel pointed out that the reader is expected to 'accept a metaphysics that she barely spells out or defends if we are to understand any of the essential distinctions she makes.'[43] What is the unstated ground of Arendt's distinctions within the *vita activa*? I want to look briefly at selected commentaries to show how eclectic were the responses to this question posed implicitly by *The Human Condition*. Then we can turn to Arendt's earlier writings on philosophy and politics prior to 1958 to see what sort of answers she might provide there to the queries raised by her critics.

John Bennett suggested that the absence of a ground of thinking, or an ontology, in Arendt's work can be explained and pardoned if we look at her within the context of 'philosophic anthropology,' this being a median ground between philosophy and science. According to Bennett, both philosophy and empiricism suffer from a restricted method of understanding. The philosopher, by definition, does not accept empirical proof as demonstrating the validity of a proposition, and the empiricist systematically excludes his own judgment from considerations of whether a proposition is true, but the philosophic anthropologist conducts a form of inquiry that is both 'empirical and valuational.'[44] The philosophic anthropologist occupies a privileged position because he can be a rational critic of phenomena and at the same time he knows that the phenomena are influenced by his own understanding. Bennett suggested that this mode of conceptualizing was one that Arendt accepted, but that she felt uncomfortable with; consequently, she strove in *The Human Condition* to overreach the limits of phenomenological understanding. Arendt failed as a critic of the modern world, in Bennett's opinion, but not because of any inherent flaw in her own argument. Rather her failure was a result of her phenomenologically 'conditioned' understanding. As an alternative to the anxious questioning of Arendt, Bennett proposed the following: 'Could we not argue with equal plausibility that it is man's nature to do these things [for example, engage in a 'mastery over nature'] and since this is so, human bio-psycho-technical evolution has been inevitable, and we must learn to use it?'[45]

Unfortunately, I think, the author's alternative to Arendt's untidy problems skirts the issues she raised. If we have difficulty understanding the world we live in, and more difficulty sorting out what is essential in the human condition from what is merely contingent, it is futile to pretend to resolve very real doubts by suppressing them or by claiming the inevitability of 'bio-psycho-technical' evolution. By dismissing the problems that Arendt raised with respect to self-understanding, Bennett succeeded only in digging himself deeper into the abyss.

This tendency to bypass the philosophical perplexities passed by *The Human Condition* is also evident in Margaret Canovan's book *The Political Thought of Hannah Arendt*. Canovan viewed Arendt as something of a romantic, who had a few insightful ideas about political action. Canovan was not concerned with exploring the ontological suppositions that were behind Arendt's distinctions, but then neither did she share Arendt's fear that the capacity for meaningful political action was influenced by changing concepts of understanding. Much more optimistic than Arendt, Canovan suggested that meaningful political action was still with us in the twentieth century in such organizations as 'churches, public houses, bowling clubs and women's institutes.'[46] She also claimed that there was such optimism in Arendt. For example, Arendt held both that action was dependent upon the proper order of labour, work, and action within the *vita activa* – and therefore was something 'only likely to be appreciated by those who are already liberated from the overwhelming pressure of bodily need and from the human bondage of slavery to a master' – and that workers' movements were 'the most hopeful sign of a possible salvation of mankind from atrophy in mass society and bureaucracy.'[47]

But Canovan's understanding of Arendt fails to distinguish between conceptual formulations (such as *animal laborans*) and reflections on real historical events. In *The Human Condition* Arendt had stated quite clearly that the only true actors in the modern world are scientists and artists, and neither of these groups can be seen as furnishing the space for a renewed political community. It is true that Arendt saw something of the spirit of action emerge in certain workers' movements, the Soviet council system, and the town meetings of New England, but it certainly was not because of the fact that the participants in these communities were labourers that they were able to act.[48] Canovan used the example of the worker's movements to show that in some cases Arendt thought that *animal laborans* was capable of action. But this is a category error, a confusion of conceptual terms with real individuals. Certain political events in the twentieth century were important to Arendt precisely because their participants were able to transcend the 'mood' of *animal laborans*. In any case, the effort was short-lived and Arendt catalogued the defeat of each one of them.[49]

What Canovan did was use examples from Arendt's writing to show how one could find what Canovan considered helpful insights into prescriptive remedies for contemporary politics, in the midst of an otherwise tragic view of history. Canovan's emphasis misrepresents the general importance of what Arendt had to say. Canovan devoted an entire chapter in her book to 'Politics and Thought,' but failed to emphasize the problems posed by the coincidence of the origins of philosophy and the demise of political action. She simply contrasted Arendt's notion of political judgment, and its association with the conditions of plurality and speech, with the 'traditional quest of philosophy and science for truth,' noting that 'one of the recurring themes of her writings is this opposition between the claims of truth and the claims of humanity.' Canovan concluded: 'The central point of her thinking is her insistence that men are unique individuals capable of original action,'[50] yet this conclusion seems to ignore the tragic tone of *The Human Condition*.

Regarding Arendt as a humanist whose work can help us recover the spirit of public action in a democracy demonstrates a faith in participatory politics that Arendt did not share. Canovan's interpretation of Arendt reminds one of Bennett's – the latter had remarked that Arendt's problem was that she was not humanistic enough. Both were willing to set aside Arendt's lengthy discussions of the traditions of philosophy as a concern separate from action, to bracket out the turgid ruminations on 'thinking,' and to turn *The Human Condition* into a handbook for modern democrats. I believe that Arendt would have found this sort of optimistic humanism a naïve understanding of the situation facing Western societies.[51]

The contemporary situation as Arendt saw it was difficult to understand and even more difficult to alter because our capacities to work, act, and think may have been fundamentally altered by the dissolution of the distinction between the *vita activa* and the *vita contemplativa*. Our immersion in process makes it hard for us to see these distinctions; and, even when we can, the recollection of them does not aid us because the problems we face stem ultimately from the origin of philosophy and the formulation of those very distinctions whose absence we might lament. We can interpret the modern situation in terms of a comparison with an ancient Greek conception, but Arendt considered the latter to be part of the problem. Accordingly, she implicitly proposed that we should attempt to think beyond the origins of rational thought itself. Canovan was undoubtedly correct in saying that action, not thought, was Arendt's expressed concern in *The Human Condition*, but action in its fullest, political meaning is possible only in a world uncorrupted by thought. Action therefore is impossible in our present world. However, the absence of the conditions for action did not prevent Arendt from thinking about it.

As Alvarez, one of the critics who treated Arendt as a poet, commented, the only optimistic note to emerge from *The Human Condition* is a renewed faith in the possibility of clear thought. Arendt stands as a refutation of her own thesis. In spite of the fact that she dreaded that human existence as it had been given in the tradition was in danger of disappearing, she was able to reflect with anxiety on this state of affairs. Alvarez compared *The Human Condition* to a 'Kafka situation' in which 'the protagonist is always an intelligent, human, three-dimensional person who suddenly finds himself thrust into a two-dimensional world.'[52] The solution to the problems raised in the book lies not in any political reform, which would be an awesome task, but in the example of Arendt herself whose 'free, serenely mature and disinterested intelligence' is testimony to the possibility that one can still think in a 'three-dimensional way' even though one has been born into a 'two-dimensional' world.

Although one might draw inspiration from the example of Hannah Arendt, the task of the theorist is greater than mute appreciation. One still has to try to comprehend the grounds on which Arendt could sustain this clarity of thought. Mildred Bakan confronted this question directly in an article entitled 'Hannah Arendt's Concepts of Labour and Work.'[53] I will outline her argument here: its open-ended conclusion leads directly into the topic of the next section of this chapter.

Bakan's article begins with a summary of Hannah Arendt's concepts of labour and work. Her subsequent argument is divided into two distinct parts. In the first segment, Bakan discusses her own understanding of the origins of consciousness in the dialectical relationship between master and slave. This dialectical relationship expands into a philosophy of history in which 'labour is the concretely material relation of man to nature by virtue of which man surpasses instinctual determination, and, also, makes that world (through work) where he must find himself.'[54] The notion that labour makes the world and is the activity through which man surpasses instinctual determination is, of course, one that Arendt disagreed with, and that has its origin in the theories of Hegel and Marx. Bakan, then, established her own affinity with the Marxist-Hegelian tradition in order to contrast it with Arendt's understanding.

Bakan rightly identified Arendt's categories of the human condition with Aristotle's conception of the *polis* as the realm of freedom, labour as the realm of necessity.[55] Most important for Bakan's concerns, Arendt and Aristotle both thought that labour was a necessary and burdensome activity, and a pre-condition for the exercise of freedom. However, Aristotle and Plato claimed that their knowledge of these distinctions came from their noetic grasp of the divine ground of being which was, for them, the 'paradigm for both the state and the soul.'[56] The philosopher understands the necessary order of activities within the *polis*, just as he understands the necessary order of the passions of the soul and the order of the cosmos itself. Bakan rejects the Platonic-Aristotelian explanation for the origins of thought. She was puzzled by how a philosopher such as Aristotle, who qua human being is part of nature, could grasp all of nature in its divine plan, and translate that into a knowledge of the necessary order of political life. None the less, Bakan acknowledged that such an understanding is a respected part of the Western philosophical tradition.

The difficulty we encounter with Arendt's formulations, then, is that while she accepted the Platonic-Aristotelian distinctions among work, labour, and political action or freedom, she did not ground these distinctions in anything like the ancient philosophical understanding of the whole.[57] Without a conception of the divine ground of order, Arendt's rigid formulations appear to have no basis. At the same time, she rejected what one might call the historicist view of the dialectical relationship between labour and freedom. She persisted in defending the autonomy of *animal laborans* and *homo faber*, and the separation of both from the political actor, but without specifying the ontological status of these activities in any comprehensive manner. The result is that, for Arendt, 'freedom seemed to be unfounded caprice.'[58]

Is it possible that Arendt conceived political action, or freedom, as an aesthetic engagement, detached from all considerations of purpose, meaning, or judgment? I think not. Arendt was well versed in the tradition of political thought, and had studied with some of the great thinkers of the twentieth century. She was fully aware of the problems inherent in considerations of justice and politics, but chose to reject the tradition of political thought in its entirety precisely because she thought that it no longer provided man with the requisite means for understanding these problems. In 1950 Arendt had written that 'it should be possible to discover the hidden mechanics by which all traditional elements of our political and spiritual world were dissolved into a conglomeration where everything seems to have lost specific value, and has become unrecognizable for human comprehension, unusable for human purpose.'[59] This passage is taken from the original preface to *The Origins of Totalitarianism*, where Arendt addressed herself specifically to the concerns of the title but more generally to the problem of the tradition as a whole. As she saw it, totalitarianism means that 'the subterranean stream of Western history has finally come to the surface and usurped the dignity of our tradition.'[60] Arendt wrote extensively on this 'subterranean stream' as it was embodied in the history of thought, and gave reasons for why she rejected thought as a credible authority on the human condition. These writings provide some defence against the charges that Arendt's understanding of political action was an aesthetic notion, but it remains to be seen whether she was able to provide a convincing ontology other than that expressed within the tradition of thought. One suspects that she could not, given her cryptic comment about the saving grace of thought at the close of *The Human Condition*.

The Vita Contemplativa *and the Tradition*

As Mildred Bakan pointed out, Arendt expressly rejected both the modern historicist tradition (represented in the thought of Hegel and Marx) and the ancient philosophical tradition (Plato and Aristotle) as valid grounds for understanding the human condition, though, in many respects, her thought resembled that of Aristotle. Arendt wrote about both these traditions but there is a two-tiered structure in her method. Her critique of modern thought, which includes not just Marx and Hegel but ranges from Descartes to Heidegger, rests on a comparison with the ancient mode of understanding. There was, she thought, an essential dimension of human experience missing from all modern philosophy, but present in ancient history. Yet, Arendt contended that the ancient tradition, extending from Plato to Descartes, also had suppressed a vital aspect of experience. For this critique of ancient thought, Arendt had no earlier tradition against which to measure its merits. Instead, she compared it to her own experience of the world. This second tier of Arendt's analysis, rooted in her own understanding but attached to no theoretical basis, is the most difficult, but the most important, element in her thought. Once Arendt had pulled the ground out from under both the modern and ancient streams of thought, she was faced with the task of creating a theory of man that lay beyond the reaches of traditional discourse, whether ancient or modern. However peculiar this might seem, it was a conclusion that she arrived at after a fascinating account of the history of philosophy.

Arendt understood the tradition of political philosophy as a coherent unit that 'had its definite beginnings in Plato and Aristotle' and 'came to a no less definite end in the theories of Karl Marx.'[61] The tradition began when the philosopher turned away from politics so as to fix his gaze on things divine, and ended when 'a philosopher turned away from philosophy so as to 'realize' it in politics.'[62] It was Marx who finally inverted the traditional hierarchy of thought and action, philosophy and politics, and so brought an end to political thought as it had always been understood in Western civilization. According to Arendt, this inversion had four distinct features: (1) labour, not God, creates man; (2) man therefore creates himself; (3) what distinguishes man from animal is not reason, but labour; and (4) labour (heretofore regarded as man's most base activity) is man's most glorious achievement. Without doing an injustice to Arendt's formulations, I think we can translate these four features into three broader ones: atheism, historicism, and the decline of reason.

Taken collectively, Marx's assumptions about man lend themselves to a justification of violence in politics and a denigration of freedom in history. If man realizes *himself* in history, and history is a series of violent disruptions that provoke change, then violence must be viewed as a necessary part of human development. Following Marx's inversions, actions that traditionally were deplored by philosophers as haphazard or corrupt were sanctioned as the motor of human development. Neither reason nor God suffices, in Marx's estimation, as a legitimate ground of resistance to specific historical acts. Similarly, if the pain of labour is recognized as the most significant 'fact' of history, then freedom and spontaneity occupy no place in the annals of historical achievement. True freedom, for Marx, can occur only once violence and labour have been overcome as determinate modes of existence, and this can happen only when history has ended in the form of a world-wide proletarian revolution. Even if such an apocalyptic event were possible, Arendt said, freedom would be a hollow concept since it would represent something that is beyond the experience of man as a historical creature. She asked rhetorically of Marx:

> If labour is the most human and most productive of man's abilities, what will happen when, after the revolution, 'labour is abolished' in the 'realm of free-dom,' when man has succeeded in emancipating himself from it? What productive and essentially human activity will be left? If violence is the midwife of history, and violent action therefore the most dignified of all forms of human action, what will happen when, after the conclusion of class struggle and the disappearance of the state, no violence will even be possible? How will men be able to act at all in a meaningful, authentic way? Finally, when philosophy has been both realized and abolished, in the future society, what kind of thought will be left?[63]

These questions all pointed to what Arendt considered to be flagrant, and unresolvable, contradictions in Marx's thought. However, she praised Marx for being the only modern thinker to realize the full implications of the modern derailment of philosophy. The contradictions in Marx are ones inherent in all thought since Descartes, but not spelled out until his work. Marx, but also Nietzsche and Kierkegaard, stand at the end of the modern 'inversion.' All responded, in different ways, to the problems of atheism, historicism, and the demise of reason. Each 'foreshadowed and illuminated' the state of the world as it would appear after their deaths.[64]

If one can single out one feature that separates the modern age from the tradition as a whole, Arendt said that it would be the concept of process. The modern understanding of process 'bestow[s] upon mere time-sequence an importance and dignity it never had before.'[65] Arendt chose Marx as the exemplary theorist of process because he was the only one to acknowledge that if one attributes meaning to history as a process of development, one can understand that process fully only once it has reached its culmination. 'In this context, it is important to see that here the process of history, as it shows itself in our calendar's stretching into the infinity of the past and the future, has been abandoned for the sake of an altogether different kind of process, that of making something which has a beginning as well as an end, whose laws of motion, therefore, can be determined (for instance as dialectical movement) and whose innermost content can be discovered (for instance as class struggle).'[66]

Arendt raised two main objections to the modern preoccupation with process as inherently meaningful. First, it is not derived from any real experience of history; rather the faith in process, or in man's ability to make himself in history, arose from the early modern despair at ever knowing the real meaning of human action.[67] Secondly, if all actions are judged retrospectively in the context of the role they play in the unfolding of a necessary historical pattern, the integrity and freedom of the single act is lost.[68] The first objection, according to Arendt, can be made clear by tracing the history of thought since Descartes. Descartes, confronted with certain scientific discoveries that gave man a knowledge that he could never have achieved through sense-perception or unaided reason, was troubled by the possibility that man's 'naked senses' deceived him. Without the confidence in the 'truth-telling' capacities of the senses, neither faith in God nor trust in reason was secure. As Arendt said, 'the revelation of both divine and rational truth had always been implicitly understood to follow the awe-inspiring simplicity of man's relationship with the world. I open my eyes and behold the vision, I listen and hear the sound, I move my body and touch the tangibility of the world.'[69] The modern age ushered in the 'school of suspicion' in which we find the roots of empiricism – Hume's assertion that the meaning of reality is revealed through repeated performances, but never reveals itself essentially – and subjectivism – Vico's contention that we can know only what we make ourselves.[70] In empirical and subjective philosophies, meaning is perceived to lie in processes, rather than essences. It is as though man, despairing at ever being able to know the real meaning of things, turned to the products and thoughts of his own creation as a restricted, but secure, realm of knowing.

We have already seen the main implication of the world-domination by *animal laborans*: once process is unhinged from any meaningful end, activity degenerates into an infinite cycle of production and consumption. Marx tried to harness this infinite cycle by conceiving of a master plan in history, with a beginning and an end, but he could do so only by 'forgetting' the experience that launched theories of process in the first place: the experience of despair. Process theory reached its logical end in Marx, who tried to dispel all wonder, all anxiety, from existence. By analogy, Arendt said that it was 'as though the carpenter, for instance, forgot that only his particular acts in making a table are performed in the mode of "in order to," but that his whole life as a carpenter is ruled by something quite different, namely an encompassing notion "for the sake of" which he became a carpenter in the first place.'[71] For Marx, the whole of history could be understood 'in order to' achieve freedom, but this freedom could not be articulated in any meaningful way. *Animal laborans* could not rescue man from his worldlessness because the modern predicament has its origins in a corruption of thought. By denying the very real experience of thought and doubt Marx cut off a whole realm of experience. Without thought, which creates meaning, no 'world' is possible. The socialized men of Marx's ideal state are 'men who have decided never to leave what to Plato was "the cave" of everyday human affairs, and never to venture on their own into a world and a life which, perhaps, the ubiquitous functionalization of modern society has deprived of one of its most elementary characteristics – the instilling of wonder at that which is as it is.'[72] This passage aptly summarizes Arendt's first objection to theories of process: they deny the worth of the experience of wonder, which was at the very basis of pre-modern philosophy, and which was shaken (but not destroyed) by early modern scientific discovery.

The denial of wonder, or doubt, as a fundamental aspect of the human condition leads to the second consequence of process to which Arendt objected. Any understanding of history that reads meaning backward – that is, from the standpoint of the present as more meaningful, more 'full,' than any moment in the past – does an injustice to the free and heroic deeds of those who lived before. Arendt did not think that there was any progress in the realm of human affairs. The deeds and words of men are significant in any age insofar as they isolate the extraordinary from the mundane. The backdrop against which such deeds are performed is the realm of 'being forever,'[73] a realm whose meaning is unknown to us since it is the space into which we are born. In contrast to this realm, which remains a mystery, mortality is the 'hallmark of human existence.' Each individual has a recognizable life story that interrupts the natural, formless space of eternity. But while the hallmark of human existence is mortality (the recognition that each individual life is finite and distinctive), human existence as a whole constitutes its own particular infinity within the greater infinity of nature. Natality, or regeneration, ensures that even though each life is finite, the human species extends infinitely into the past and the future.[74] 'The individual life is distinguished from all other things by the rectilinear course of its movement, which, so to speak, cuts through the circular movements of biological life.'[75]

The chain of human lives, and the cycle of nature, are the two realms of 'being forever' against which all human endeavour is undertaken. For Hannah Arendt, the deeds and events that stand out against these continuums are what constitute meaningful history. The task of the poet or historiographer is to remember these luminous moments, without corrupting their inherent worthiness by attributing them to the workings of either realm of infinitude. Arendt also knew that this was a lot to ask of those who record great deeds and events. Since the grand gesture, the magnanimous act are but fleeting moments in an otherwise overwhelming continuum of life, the temptation is great to measure them against the much more stable realms of 'being forever.'[76] The temptation can lead, as it did in the modern age, to assigning to acts and words a meaning that transcends the particularity of their expression and assimilates them to some historical pattern. 'History – based on the manifest assumption that no matter how haphazard single actions may appear in the present and in their singularity, they inevitably lead to a sequence of events forming a story that can be rendered through intelligible narrative the moment the events are removed into the past – became the great dimension in which men could become "reconciled" with reality (Hegel), the reality of human affairs, i.e., of things which owe their existence exclusively to men.'[77] The great error of historicist thought lay in its treating the single event, the free act, as a manifestation of the linear continuum of human (species) infinitude. All meaning was thus construed as originating in the chain of life and labour. This reduction of the particular act to its role in the march of time destroyed the glory of action.

Modern process theory reduced all experience to the linear concept of time, thus denying 'wonder at that which is' as well as the integrity of the single act: but ancient philosophy committed an equally grievous mistake, according to Arendt. It reduced all experience to man's participation in the cyclical infinity of nature, thus neglecting the importance of linear infinitude as well as the particular act. When confronted with the 'paradox' of perishable human deeds in the unperishable order of nature, Plato turned away from the transience of human affairs. The orientation of the philosopher, as he understood it, was 'to dwell in the neighbourhood of those things which are forever, to be there and present in a state of active attention, but without doing anything.'[78] Turning away from things human, Plato constructed all of human life 'in the image of biological life.'[79] 'In terms of ancient philosophy, this could mean that the world of history had been reintegrated into the world of nature, the world of mortals into the universe that is forever.'[80] What we now acknowledge as the essential experience behind the activity of philosophizing was, for the ancient Greek thinkers, the 'quiet, actionless, selfless contemplation of the miracle of being.'

Arendt thought that philosophy had been 'discovered' at the expense of great deeds and action, and at the expense of a respect for temporal existence. Philosophy strove to make man in the image of the divine at the price of immortal recognition in this human realm. For the missing link in ancient thought – that is, the respect for regeneration, species continuity, and history – Arendt referred back to the historicist tradition that she denounced. It appears, then, that there is a vicious circle within the tradition: at no point in it do the three dimensions of existence – (1) the cyclical, natural infinitude, (2) the linear, temporal infinitude, and (3) the particular act – come together in a harmonious way. One dimension of 'eternity' is always emphasized to the detriment of the other and in the process the importance of the single deed suffers. In examining the *vita activa*, Arendt wanted to exclude the entire tradition of Western thought because it appeared to be incapable of expressing the full reality of human experience.

Superficially, it seems that Arendt romanticized the tragic existence of the Greek hero. She often referred to Achilles as an example of one who was able to act courageously, in spite of the fact that he knew his actions were unable to alter the given order of things. Arendt blamed Plato for being the first to flee this human paradox, or tragedy, but on closer examination, it seems that she held thought in itself as responsible for the flight from the world's uncertainty. There seemed to her to be something inherent in the faculty of thought that makes it turn away from the contingencies of the world and try to integrate the unexpected and the extraordinary acts of men into a systematic whole. Even the historian is guilty of attributing sequential meaning to the past. For Arendt, rescuing man from the pitfalls of the Western tradition depended upon our ability to, in effect, think beyond the imperatives of thought. She once remarked: 'I have always believed that, no matter how abstract our theories may sound or how consistent our arguments may appear, there are incidents and stories behind them which, at least for ourselves, contain as in a nutshell the full meaning of whatever we have to say.'[81] In keeping with this statement, Arendt believed that the experience that led to philosophical inquiry was the paradox and uncertainty of human life; therefore, it is the experience of this uncertainty that ought to be our guide-post, and not the theoretical solutions that arose from it. Similarly, historicist thought is rooted in the feeling of despair associated with scientific discovery and the subsequent loss of faith in the revelatory capacities of the senses. It is the experience of doubt and despair that we ought to remember is the ground of all modern 'process' theory. If we return to these incidents behind the theories, Arendt suggested, we may be able to arrive at a better understanding of the world than that passed to us by the tradition.

Returning to fundamental experiences was especially important in the twentieth century since thought had wandered off into unprecedented directions in our time. Arendt thought the waywardness of thought could be traced back to its origins in the mood of despair caused by the onslaught of science at the beginning of the modern age. The rejection of 'wonder' as an inadequate form of knowing led to an ill-conceived desire on the part of humanity to see itself as self-created. After the collapse of the tradition (marked definitively by Marx's writings), thinkers explored this proposition, and ended by making what Arendt considered to be absurd and dangerous claims about the nature of existence. She discussed the history of this 'post-traditional' thought in an article entitled 'What Is Existenz Philosophy?'[82]

Just as Arendt chose a pivotal figure to represent ancient philosophy (Plato) and one to characterize modern thought (Marx), so too she pointed to a 'secret king' of existenz philosophy: Kant. Arendt claimed that Kant made clear what was only an air of foreboding in Descartes, that is, that there is no unity between being and thought. Human beings are capable of thinking things that are untrue (such as 'the earth is flat') and they are incapable of thinking the noumenal, or essential, reality of things. Kant seemed to be quite comfortable with this conclusion, and resolved what appeared to be an impasse with the proposition that what the rational mind cannot know, it posits as an ideal of reason.[83] However, this resolution was clearly unacceptable to later thinkers, for whom the notion that reason assumes there is some reality behind its insights was an inadequate form of understanding. These later thinkers rejected reason altogether as the clue to knowing 'Being' and turned instead to sheer existence. In this respect, they catgegorically rejected the tradition of thought. Marx was the last in the tradition because he was the last to understand being rationally. He tried to discover reason in history, which is different from the ancient understanding of reason grounded in divine *nous*, but none the less the emphasis is on a rational grasp of meaning. In contrast, the existenz philosophers released man from his grounding in both historical continuum and the participation in divine order, and conceived of him as a free-floating, unbounded 'existenz.' Kierkegaard, one of the earliest existenz thinkers, celebrated this independent life-force as the only source of meaning for man. Arendt reiterated his position as follows: 'This Existenz, which I am continually but momentarily, and which I cannot grasp by Reason, is the only thing of which I can be absolutely certain. Thus, man's task is to "become subjective," a consciously existing being who perpetually realizes the paradoxical implications of his life in the world.'[84] But, she continued, the emphasis on Existenz did not imply a simple 'yea to life or to the human reality of man as such,' for in turning to sheer life as the ground of meaning, the existenz philosophers also had to come to terms with the incontrovertible fact of death. Death is the main obstacle to free, 'subjective' reality. In the natural movement of every living being towards death, subjective freedom cannot be maintained. Hence, later existenz philosophers – notably Heidegger – became preoccupied with death as a challenge to absolute human freedom. Heidegger met this challenge by asserting that since death is the main impediment to subjective freedom, we cannot maintain that freedom is the 'essence' of human life. Rather, the actual meaning of life is death. Being is Nothingness. Arendt was unequivocal in her judgment about Heidegger at this point. She commented that his theoretical conclusions about existence bore a relation to his political affiliation with the Nazi party and called him the last romantic. His 'complete irresponsibility' she attributed 'partly to the delusion of genius, partly to desperation.'[85] In portraying being as nothing, Heidegger attempted to resist the responsibility that man has to the 'given' limits of human capacities. 'The Nothing tries, so to speak, to reduce to nothing, the giveness of Being, and to put itself in Being's place.'[86] This, thought Arendt, was nihilism.

The political consequences of a world-view such as Heidegger's are devastating. If the reality of man's being is conceived as 'nothingness,' and the ultimate achievement of life is the passage into the void (death), then life among one's fellow human beings can have no real significance. By virtue of the fact that a man even exists, he is thereby controverting his 'true' nature. In this case, suicide would seem to be a noble form of action, although it did not appear to be so for Heidegger (as it could be for other modern, existentialist philosophers, such as Camus). For Heidegger, the Self lives in an encompassing mood of guilt, guilt at defying his true being, or his nothingness. As such, existence strives to be as autonomous as possible: not to be lured into webs of false meaning that might take the form of community or religion, or any other form of life-affirming activity. Heidegger arrived at his ideal of the 'Self', according to Arendt, by making man into a radically autonomous creature: 'a unique individual being who knows no equals.' For Heidegger, 'the worst essential characteristic of this Self is its absolute egoism, its radical separation from all its fellows.'[87]

For Arendt, Heidegger was the extreme example of thought gone mad. Unwilling to accept the necessary limitations to reason, or the 'mute' understanding that is common to most men who do not suffer existentially under the burden of mortality, Heidegger pushed thought to its most desperate conclusions. He tried to rely solely on thought to reconcile the diremption between Being and thought, and ended by denying the substance of both. Contrary to the claims made by existenz philosophy – that it relies on existence, not thought, for truth – what it really does is forsake the given-ness of being for the abstraction of pure thought. At this juncture, I believe some comparison of Heidegger with Plato is in order, even though Arendt did not draw the comparison in her article on existenz philosophy.

Both Plato and Heidegger began philosophizing with the assumption that the meaning of life can be understood only in the awareness of death. Arendt thought both were wrong in making this assumption, but also contended that Heidegger's thought ended in madness whereas Plato's did not. The distance between Heidegger and Plato is huge because, for Heidegger, philosophy was about death, which is to say about nothing, while for Plato, philosophy turned to death as the expression of man's entry into the divine order of nature. In short, Heidegger was an atheist and Plato was not. By attaching philosophy to the existence of a hidden, given order of being, Plato could accept the given limits of human reason. This kept him from traversing the boundaries of common sense, but his understanding of truth as accessible to the philosopher after death led him to turn away from the community of living men and towards the yearning of the soul. Plato, then, was able to save his own soul, but at the price of meaningful participation in the pluralistic, political world of living men. Heidegger was unable truthfully to find meaning either in the depths of his own soul or in the community of his fellow men. In an atheistic world, excessive thinking on Heidegger's part pushed him over the brink into nihilism.

Madness comes from excessive abstraction, not from atheism per se. We must remember that Arendt criticized Plato precisely for his having dwelled on eternal, rather than temporal, matters. Arendt thought it was possible to live in an atheistic world and still be able to recognize the given-ness of being. One need not agree with Heidegger's conclusions. In fact, Arendt went further to suggest that the contemporary (post-traditional) world afforded man a unique opportunity to start over, to begin a new and better tradition unfettered by any of the philosophical baggage of the past. This new beginning, for her, required that one 'give oneself' over to Being. Here, as elsewhere, she had a specific example of a thinker who elaborated such a possibility – Karl Jaspers, her own teacher. She summarized the foundations of his philosophy as follows:

> The question concerning the That of reality, which cannot be resolved into thought, acquires a new meaning without losing its character as real. The That of Being as the given – whether as the reality of the world, as the incalculability of one's fellow men, or the fact that I have not created myself – becomes the backdrop against which man's freedom emerges, becomes at the same time the stuff which kindles it. That I cannot resolve the real to the object of thought becomes the triumph of possible freedom. In this context, the question concerning the meaning of Being can be so suspended that the answer to it runs: 'Being is such that this human reality is possible.'[88]

For Jaspers and for Arendt (at this point) thinking performs the task of leading man back to the experience of the world at which point thought fails. Independent thought can never give a complete account of the diverse and unpredictable realm of human affairs. It is in the 'foundering of thought' in the midst of this complexity that existence reveals itself as a truly mysterious thing.[89] Jaspers's recognition that one cannot 'resolve the real to the object of thought' was, for Arendt, a major breakthrough in the history of thought. It was as if the world had been liberated from what Arendt called the 'Ghost of Being,' or at least from the compulsion to explain Being theoretically. What Arendt admired most about Jaspers's philosophy was the possibilities that it opened up for a renewed faith in the revelatory capacity of politics. Once Being is re-embraced as a given, men can direct their energies towards creating a meaningful *human* world. Thus, 'we at least arrive at the conclusion that Man as "Master of his thoughts" not only is more than any of his thoughts (and this would probably be the most fundamental condition for a new definition of human dignity), but that from the first man's nature is to be more than himself and to will more than himself.'[90]

The notion that man can 'will more than himself' as a given, natural entity still poses some difficulty for understanding, however. Arendt contrasted Jaspers with Heidegger, saying that these two thinkers, though both situated within the 'existenz' tradition, had radically different conceptions of the meaning of human being. Both thought the future of philosophy lay in the possibility for wilful action and thought. Both identified meaning for human beings as something different from the infinity into which human life is plunged. In saying that man is more than any of his thoughts, Arendt implied that man's actions could never be rationally understood. Action, unconstrained by reason, she knew full well could be a very dangerous weapon. If man's existence is not attached in any determinate way to the dicta of reason, how can we judge the wilful activities of men? What, indeed, keeps men from participating in unfounded caprice?

Arendt tried to answer these questions in an essay on 'Understanding and Politics.' There, she made the distinction between understanding as the mute experience of being human, and theoretical explanation. 'Understanding,' she wrote, 'is unending and therefore cannot produce end-results; it is the specifically human way of being alive ... Understanding begins with birth and ends with death.'[91] Accordingly, it is the 'preliminary, inarticulate' meaning that 'precedes and succeeds knowledge.'[92] Moreover, according to Arendt, understanding is the universal basis of common sense that is a given condition of being human. The proper task of theory is to render this given intelligible through rational speech, but this presupposes that the theorist acknowledges the limitations of rational discourse. As a counterweight to the tyranny of thought in the Western tradition, Arendt appealed to this universal common sense. Citing the example of King Solomon's prayer to God for an 'understanding heart,' she appealed to the substance of that prayer as a clue to the means of overcoming the theoretical impasse of the modern world. Solomon, 'who certainly knew something of political action, addressed God for the gift of an "understanding heart" as the greatest gift a man could receive and desire.'[93] In our secular, atheistic age, Arendt said, we can translate this religious appeal for an understanding heart into the universal appeal to all men to exercise the 'faculty of the imagination.'[94] This 'faculty,' she stated, is not the faculty of thought, but the 'inner compass' that anchors thought. It is directed towards the community of men, in whom and through whom it acquires its universal status. Through dialogue and participation with others, the 'darkness of the human heart' is illuminated. The sharing of experience is of paramount importance to Arendt, for it is only in testing our thoughts against the experiences of others that we can find out whether they make sense or are fantastic creations of a deluded mind. And this is why, for her, meaning is intrinsically tied to the political world. A shared space, a political arena for the exchange of ideas, is essential to her understanding of the human condition. Action, with its attendant conditions of speech and plurality, is the mode through which meaning is given substantial reality.

But we have seen in Arendt's own account that this conception of the origins of meaning has never been accepted as entirely adequate. The world of action has never been considered by serious thinkers to be properly constitutive of meaning, since it is a volatile, unpredictable, and unstable realm. From the time of Plato, philosophers have tended to retreat from political life. Looking at the biographies of philosophers, one is hard pressed to find even a few who *actively* sought to enter politics for the gratification of taking part in public debate. One might be tempted, then, to view all of the past in terms of two parallel developments: the history of thought and the history of action. In that case, the solution to Arendt's problem would be simple: forget the philosophers and look to the world of common sense for meaning. Unfortunately, the annals of thought are not so detached from the record of actual events. As Arendt said, 'It would be folly indeed to overlook the almost too precise congruity of modern man's world alienation with the subjectivism of modern philosophy,'[95] and it would be equally foolish 'to believe that our world would have become different if only philosophy had held fast to tradition.'[96] Thought and 'real history' are interconnected to the extent that it is the living person who engages in both. Thought may take strange directions in the hands of 'professional thinkers,' but there is no doubt that it is a fundamental capacity of all people. One cannot therefore treat the philosopher as though he were some extraterrestrial being whose shortcomings are anomalous to most of humanity. On the contrary, he probably expresses in a highly articulate way what is common to his world.

The bond between thought and action is something that Arendt was aware of, but seemed to resist. (In this respect, the criticism of the 'philosophic anthropologist' is correct.) In a world that has a history of violence and cruelty, I think she sometimes resented the retreat of the philosopher. She regarded it in some manner as an abdication of one's responsibility to other men.[97] She believed in the inherent capacity of human beings to know justice, meaning, and morality when they saw it, but found little evidence of such awareness in history. In her most sullen moods, she blamed thought – not just in philosophers, but in all men – for forsaking these capacities. The twentieth century appeared to her to be an especially gloomy time because these capacities had all but disappeared. Under the impact of totalitarianism, it seemed that the 'understanding heart' had withered away completely. Its existence had already been threatened by the direction of modern philosophy, which denied its reality, but in an actual state whose motivating principle was total domination, the conditions for understanding – that is, the toleration of free speech and action – had been eradicated. This is why Arendt feared that in the twentieth century 'human nature as such is at stake.'[98]

Yet Arendt did not defend this claim consistently in her work. When she elaborated her own understanding of meaning, as it was shaped by her faith in the capacity for political action, she realized that in the absence of the conditions for free speech and action, some people were still capable of good judgment. In spite of the fact that all of the 'backdrops' for understanding had been demolished under totalitarianism, and therefore, according to Arendt's own methodology, human nature had been jeopardized, *individual* people were able to exercise free thought. As a consequence of her reflections on totalitarianism, and especially of her analysis of the trial of Adolf Eichmann, Arendt came to realize that good judgment, or an understanding heart, did not depend for its presence on the conditions of plurality and speech. This realization, in turn, led her to refute her earlier claim that ethical behaviour was intrinsically bound to forms of political organization.[99] And, eventually, it drew her back to considerations of the very tradition she had rejected.

Thus far, I have tried to summarize Hannah Arendt's thoughts on the history of philosophy, its encroachment on the human condition, and her reasons for rejecting the tradition of thought as a legitimate basis for understanding the world. I have also tried to isolate her thoughts on an alternative mode of understanding: the 'faculty of the imagination' as she saw it expressed in the work of Karl Jaspers. I have already suggested that this alternative mode is inadequate to express certain kinds of behaviour in the twentieth century, but I think this becomes increasingly evident when we look at what Arendt had to say about political events, rather than theories, in the twentieth century. Through her analysis of totalitarianism, and her effort to understand the motives of those who actively took part in its success, those who remained passive, and those who resisted, she came to see that 'intersubjective community' was no guarantee of free, responsible action. Nor did its absence mean that freedom and responsibility had fled the world. Individuals were capable of independent judgment under conditions of extreme duress, and this appeared to have something to do with their ability to think. Thought may be man's most accursed 'gift' since it can lure him into destructive fantasy, but it is also man's redemptive capacity. Arendt had written at the close of *The Human Condition*: 'Thought, finally – which we, following the premodern as well as the modern tradition, omitted from our reconsideration of the *vita activa* – is still possible, and no doubt actual, wherever men live under the conditions of political freedom.'[100] Much later, in *The Life of the Mind*, she was to write: 'Could the activity of thinking as such, the habit of examining whatever happens to come to pass or to attract attention, regardless of results and specific content, could this activity be among the conditions that make men abstain from evil-doing or even "condition" them againsxt it?'[101] The contrast between these two passages is striking. By the 1970s Arendt had seriously considered the possibility that her earlier conviction, namely that thought grows out of the *vita activa*, was wrong; that, in fact, thought may be among those qualities in human beings that shape or resist the character of the *vita activa*. However, there is much to be considered before we turn to this final statement by Arendt. The next chapter will concern itself with her reflections on twentieth-century politics, a subject that occupied at least as much space in her collected writings as her thoughts on 'thinking.'

2 Acting in the Realm of Appearances

Totalitarianism, Terror, and Ideology

In chapter 1, I cited a passage from Hannah Arendt in which she made the general claim that behind every theory there are incidents and stories that 'contain as in a nutshell the full meaning of whatever we have to say.' In light of this remark one might say that the most important 'incident' behind Arendt's theory is the twentieth-century experience of totalitarianism. She commented on more than one occasion that the experience of living in, and fleeing from, Nazi Germany was the formative experience of her life.

In the preface to the first edition of *The Origins of Totalitarianism*, Arendt commented that as a consequence of events under the rule of Stalin and Hitler our future is 'unpredictable,' our political forces 'look like sheer insanity,' and 'the essential structure of all civilizations is at the breaking point.'[1] The fact that totalitarianism is a form of *action*, and not merely speculative thought, makes it a much more urgent matter than the state of philosophy in the modern world. We already know from our discussion of *The Human Condition* and other writings that Arendt considered any form of action a product of spontaneous, wilful endeavour. While one cannot isolate the acts of human beings from their thoughts, action none the less occupies an antecedent priority in the scheme of history. It is the 'stuff' of civilization upon which all theory rests. The story of totalitarianism, as Arendt understood it, revealed a new political experience and therefore required a new mode of understanding. As she put it, the acts committed in totalitarian regimes have 'exploded the very alternative on which all definitions of the essence of governments have been based in political philosophy, that is the alternative between lawful and lawless government, between arbitrary and legitimate power.'[2]

Arendt tried to provide evidence for these claims in her study of totalitarianism.

Her book is concerned with two tasks: the first, to catalogue the particular features of totalitarian rule; the second, to give an account of the intellectual roots of this form of political organization. The first task is crucial for rendering an accurate factual picture of the phenomenon, but the second is more important for political theory. In trying to understand why totalitarianism happened, in addition to describing what it was, Arendt asserted that the essential human experiences had changed in the twentieth century. Totalitarianism for her was the political expression of a qualitatively different kind of human being.

Speaking of the functional apparatus of the totalitarian state, Arendt is not the best source of information. The classic text on the specific features of totalitarian government is probably *Totalitarian Dictatorship and Autocracy* by Carl Friedrich and Zbigniew Brzezinski.[3] In their study these authors wrote about the unique characteristics of totalitarian rule in terms of its peculiar understanding of dictatorship, party organization, propaganda and police activity, economic policies, and international relations. Arendt's objective in studying totalitarianism was more ambitious, however.[4] The title of her inquiry, with its emphasis on origins, suggests the nature of her enterprise. Arendt claimed that the origins of totalitarianism were both inherent in certain historical precedents and an expression of wilful action. Totalitarianism can be understood in part by looking back at certain developments in Western European history, but its rise can never be attributed solely to these historical patterns.

This ambivalent attitude towards the origins of totalitarianism comes as no surprise given what we already know about Arendt's methods in *The Human Condition*. It was an abiding feature of this method to engage in careful historical analysis and at the same time reject it as an insufficient explanation for any phenomenon. The analysis of historical forces can help us understand the context in which totalitarianism emerged, but it cannot tell us why specific individuals took decisions to commit particular atrocities against their fellows, just as the psycho-history of a demented person cannot explain fully why that individual might have committed a criminal act.[5]

In spite of Arendt's own objections to historians who posit causal connections between past events and present ones, a large part of *The Origins* was concerned with connecting totalitarianism to prior developments. Significant among these, according to her, were the growth of anti-Semitism, nationalism, and imperialism in the centuries before the eighteenth and nineteenth. This is the focus of parts 1 and 2 of *The Origins*. The concluding part of the book, entitled 'Totalitarianism,' addresses itself to concerns of moral responsibility and individual choice. It is this part of her study that concerns us here, for it is only in this part that she attempted to come to terms with the relationship between human self-understanding in the twentieth century and the ability (or inability) of men to act in humanly accptable ways.

If we look at Arendt's analysis of totalitarianism as a whole, we find that she seemed to be saying two contradictory things: that men are responsible for totalitarianism because all political choices are human, deliberate ones; and that they are blameless because circumstances in Germany and Russia under Hitler and Stalin made it difficult for individuals to make choices of any kind. Apart from the broad historical precedents of anti-Semitism, nationalism, and imperialism, each of which contributed to specific features of totalitarianism, there were other conditions that figure prominently in its success. One of these was the use of terror. The role played by the secret police in totalitarian states made it possible to control the lives of human beings to a greater extent than ever before. 'Terror,' Arendt wrote, 'is the very essence of [the totalitarian] form of government.'[6] Terror destroys the public space entirely because it can literally prevent people from communicating with one another. Without the freedom to share their fears and concerns people are coerced by terror into the maddening isolation of their own thoughts or into the mute obedience of a mass.

The effects of terror on a whole population can be seen as similar to the effects that isolated thought can have on the modern thinker. We recall Arendt's criticisms of Heidegger. He was a man who thought his own way into nihilism as a result of his self-imposed exile from his fellow men and his attempt to arrive at a definition of man that disregards man's 'natural' home in the pluralistic world. 'To put it historically,' Arendt wrote, 'Heidegger's Self is an ideal which has been working mischief in German philosophy and literature since Romanticism. In Heidegger this arrogant passion to will to be a Self has contradicted itself; for never before was it so clear as in his philosophy that this is probably the one being which Man cannot be.'[7] What man cannot be, according to Arendt, is an autonomous 'Self.' Heidegger's delusion in thinking that he could formulate a concept of the Self without considering man's formative development in the plurality led him to what Arendt considered to be a fundamental distortion of the human condition: he tried to define the 'essence' of man in the context of radical subjectivity. Heidegger's conception of man denigrates 'all those modes of human existence which rest on the fact that Man lives together in the world with his fellows.'[8] The effects of terror in a totalitarian state, isolating human beings and preventing them from participating in any kind of intersubjective plurality, showed in a sense the *practical* consequences of treating human beings as isolated entities. 'Total domination,' Arendt said, 'strives to organize the infinite plurality and differentiation of human beings as if all of humanity were just one individual.'[9] The destruction of plurality in a totalitarian state forces a condition of lonely subjectivity on the individual, a loneliness that Arendt compared to the solitude that is an integral part of the activity of philosophizing. She commented that 'solitary men have always been in danger of loneliness, when they can no longer find the redeeming grace of companionship to save them from duality and equivocality and doubt.'[10] It seems that at this point Arendt held fast to her belief that extreme loneliness and subjectivity, whether induced by thought or by the domination of a totalitarian state, distort the capacities of the human condition.

We know that Arendt thought that some kind of public interaction was essential, not only for the existence of politics, but also for sane thought. The faculty of the imagination, that crucial capacity that is the ground for all rational judgment, requires interaction with others to flourish. It is in and through the community of free-thinking individuals that we affirm our human being. Deprived of public discussion, individuals lose something fundamental or at least something historically recognized. Under the duress of terror they become something other than human. This is what Arendt meant in saying that human nature was at stake in the twentieth century.

In fact, Arendt was not as pessimistic as some of her statements might imply. There are at least two objections that can be advanced to challenge her assertion that human nature has been altered by totalitarianism. First, we can raise the question of whether it is actually possible for any state to exert total control over every aspect of human existence. If 'human nature' depends for its existence upon some shared space for human communication, Arendt must show that totalitarian states negate absolutely the possibility for spontaneous human interaction. Any claim that totalitarianism is a unique form of political organization rests on this proof. Many writers on the subject of totalitarianism have agreed that what distinguishes it from other forms of authoritarianism such as tyranny or dictatorship is its ability and desire to exercise total control over every person's conscience. Tyrannies and dictatorships traditionally have not interfered with the private pursuits of citizens unless those pursuits were a direct threat to the security of the regime. As Hans Buchheim wrote, even though the features characteristic of authoritarian states, such as open force and the deprivation of freedom, are found in both tyrannies and totalitarian states, totalitarianism's 'true characteristic is the creeping assault on men through the perversion of thought and social life.'[11] In order to show that totalitarianism does indeed differ from all other forms of authoritarian rule it must be shown that the former destroys the individual's capacity for speaking and acting with others.

There is one sense, however, in which the discussion of the degree to which a regime invades the private space of the individual begs the real question. Theoretically it seems possible to tyrannize over every aspect of an individual's life. But even if this possibility were actualized (which it may or may not have been under Hitler and Stalin), the question remains: Is it possible to alter human nature through political coercion?

The second challenge to Arendt aims at her notion that a minimum of political freedom, or opportunity for exchange of ideas, is essential for exercising the human capacity for moral judgment and reason. Arendt's fear of totalitarianism, her concern that our categories of thought have been 'exploded,' resulted from her firm belief that free and open discussion is the origin of meaning for human beings. If that opportunity for speech is denied (which Arendt claimed is the case under totalitarian rule), then we can only conclude that the potential for critical judgment, virtuous behaviour, and rational thought has been lost. Alternatively, we can disagree with Arendt's claim that plural relations among people are the necessry condition for the emergence of these human qualities. If human beings are capable of making good judgments independent of the conditions under which they live, then our concerns are not as grave as Arendt sometimes thought they ought to be. We would not be in danger of losing our 'natures' and we would not have to abandon all our categories of thought. That 'nature' itself is not in jeopardy does not mean that the issue of totalitarianism is of any less concern to political theorists. The fact that so many people participated in such a repressive form of political life is important, though perhaps difficult to understand. But we need not infer from this fact that the essence of human beings has been altered fundamentally.

To retreat from the hypothetical to the actual, I suggested earlier, in the context of the first objection to Arendt's thesis, that it would be difficult to prove that any state exerted total control over all of its citizens. It seems that there are always islands of private resistance, no matter what the extent of terror and domination.[12] One can argue that this is a result either of inefficiency on the part of the state or of the insatiable will of some men who, in any situation, always resist repression. It is impossible to prove either of these points empirically. What matters is that even under the most severe repression in totalitarian states some men have resisted. Totalitarianism's consequences for thinking and its consequences for politics are two different things, as is made poignantly clear in the testimony of Alexander Solzhenitsyn. He observed that totalitarianism has a devastating effect on political community for the same reasons that Arendt articulated: its ban on the exchange of opinions. 'The prolonged absence of any free exchange of information within a country opens up a gulf of incomprehension between whole groups of the population, between millions and millions. We simply *cease to be a single people*, for we speak, indeed, different languages.'[13] Yet we also have Solzhenitsyn's conviction that in such a milieu it is still possible for an individual to tell right from wrong, relying on nothing more than his own isolated experiences: 'it was only when I lay there on rotting prison straw that I sensed within myself the first stirrings of good. Gradually it was disclosed to me that the line separating good and evil passes not through states, nor between classes, nor between political parties either – but right through every human heart – and through all human hearts.'[14]

Regardless of whether the distinction between good and evil is arrived at through intersubjective communication or through the experience of the heart's depths, the fact remains that few people were capable of distinguishing good from evil under the stress of totalitarian rule. How could it have been that there was such a huge abyss between our conventional understanding of justice and freedom and the practices of totalitarian states? It requires more than just brute terror to obscure 'reality' to such an extent. It requires that people are somehow willing to forsake their 'common sense' understanding of things for something that is more persuasive. Ideologies, according to Arendt, perform just such a function by substituting a set of logical deductions from an axiomatic premise for the arbitrariness and unpredictability of the real world. She referred to the explanatory device of ideological thinking as a 'strait jacket of logic': 'The danger in exchanging the necessary insecurity of philosophical thought for the total explanation of an ideology and its *Weltanschauung*, is not even so much the risk of falling for some usually vulgar, always uncritical assumption as of exchanging the freedom inherent in man's capacity to think for the strait jacket of logic with which man can force himself almost as violently as he is forced by some outside power.'[15] In some respects the ideological element in totalitarian states was more frightening to Arendt than the tgerror, for the role that ideology plays depends upon a certain amount of wilful submission. The success of ideology in a totalitarian state could never have been assured had there not been a latent predisposition towards it in the masses.

Arendt considered the emergence of mass society in the modern period to be one of the most important historical developments to precede the phenomenon of the totalitarian state, a development without which ideology could not have played its major role in totalitarianism. Mass society grew out of the dissolution of traditional class stratification. Membership in a specific class, despite all the implications that it had for hindering democratic politics, meant that one had particular interests to protect, and these interests were the bases for political organization. The disintegration of class boundaries at the turn of the twentieth century led to the simultaneous dissolution of party politics based on self-interest, according to Arendt: 'The fall of protecting class walls transformed the slumbering majorities behind all parties into one great unorganized, structureless mass of furious individuals.'[16] The political disposition of the masses is marked by two prominent features: (1) masses do not express any coherent notion of self-interest, and (2) because of their lack of commitment to specific interests, masses are susceptible to the persuasion of ideological propaganda. 'The term masses applies only where we deal with people who either because of sheer numbers, or indifference, or a combination of both, cannot be integrated into any organization based on common interest, into political parties or municipal governments, or professional organizations or trade unions.'[17] To the masses, who have no articulate loyalties or goals, ' "the ice-cold reasoning" and the "mighty tentacle" of dialectics which "seizes you as in a vise" appears like a last support in a world where nobody is reliable and nothing can be relied upon.'[18]

Arendt did dissociate the ideological elements of mass movements and of totalitarian states from ideological theories of the nineteenth century. As she was always warning, philosophical ideas are never responsible for political conditions in the world, and the ideological theories of Marx and Darwin are no exception in this regard. Still, she maintained that 'the real nature of all ideologies was revealed only in the role that ideology plays in the apparatus of totalitarian domination.'[19] Three principal concerns dominate Arendt's thoughts on ideology. First of all, all ideological theories claim to be able to do provide a *total* explanation: they claim to understand fully the patterns of the past, and on the basis of that understanding to be able to predict the future. This alleged capacity to control history, of course, directly contravenes Arendt's belief that all human action is unpredictable. Secondly, ideologies claim that these patterns, though decipherable, are hidden or masked by propaganda. For example, Marx claimed that the 'key' to history was understanding the basis of class struggle, even though history may ordinarily be understood as the rise and fall of nations, of great leaders, and so on. This second aspect of ideology troubled Arendt because it meant exchanging the obvious and visible for some meaning that is not apparent in ordinary experience. A third characteristic of ideology that Arendt disliked was its suppression of all experience under the logic deduced from a single, a priori premiss. Ideology assumes an axiomatic premiss and subsequently distorts all data and facts in such a way that they can be deduced from the single idea. 'Once it has established its premiss, its point of departure,' she wrote, 'experiences no longer interfere with ideological thinking, nor can it be taught by reality.'[20] It is this third characteristic of ideology that Arendt feared most, for the logical deductions of ideology, when applied in practice in a totalitarian state, soon lose sight of the premiss from which they were originally deduced, and the logic takes on a life of its own.

The willingness to accept the ideological elements of a totalitarian state, Arendt said, can be successful only when man has degenerated into *animal laborans*, that is, when men have already become isolated and 'worldless.' A tyranny over 'labourers,' she said, 'would automatically be a rule over lonely, not only isolated, men and tend to be totalitarian.'[21] We already know from Arendt's account in *The Human Condition* what she thought about the stature of man in general in the modern period. She attributed man's decline in large part to the eclipse of the 'public space' and the blurring of the distinctions among labour, work, and action. In *The Origins of Totalitarianism*, however, her emphasis is not on the disappearance of public space as much as it is on the decline of spiritual maxims.

She commented: 'I am perfectly sure that this whole totalitarian catastrophe would not have happened if people still had believed in God, or in hell rather – that is, if there were still ultimates.'[22]

Arendt contrasted totalitarian lawfulness and its immanent ideological standards with the tradition of positive law, whose standards are transcendent: 'Totalitarian lawfulness pretends to have found a way to establish the rule of justice on earth – something which the legality of positive law admittedly could never attain.'[23] Positive law has traditionally meant legal restrictions whose reference for authority is some transcendent non-historical concept of justice. The standards of right and wrong, conceived as the divine word of God or as the customs and traditions expressing the common sentiments of men, 'are necessarily general and must be valid for a countless and unpredictable number of cases.'[24] Positive law may change according to circumstance, but its standards are constant.

Positive law has its own problems, though; according to Arendt, the most pronounced is its invocation of the 'invisible spiritual yardstick' by which human affairs are measured. The link between the spiritual, divine measure and the affairs of men is characteristic of our tradition as a whole, beginning with Plato and extending through the Judaeo-Christian formulation of God's law.[25] However, there was a time and a culture where this 'spiritual yardstick' did not apply: the founding of Rome. The Roman tradition of lawfulness, unlike the Greek and Judaeo-Christian ones, was not sustained through a pious commitment to an other-worldly concept of justice. Rather, in Rome 'religion literally meant *re-ligare*: to be tied back, obligated, to the enormous, almost superhuman and hence always legendary effort to lay the foundations, build the cornerstone, to found for eternity.'[26] The binding power of foundation served as the authority upon which Roman law received its positive power. In this one aspect of Roman culture – its roots in the act of foundation – Arendt expressed a preference for the Roman polity over the Greek one. Since it traced its legitimacy back to human action, rather than locating it in a quietistic orientation towards the divine, its allegiance to the creative power of political associations was much greater. Yet, in the context of Western history as a whole, the 'victory of the Roman spirit is really almost a miracle.'[27] The example of the Romans was not repeated in history, with the possible exception of the founding of the United States, which, for various reasons, failed to match the spirit of its predecessor. Ultimately, Rome was subsumed under the power of the Christian church because the church 'amalgamated the Roman political concept of authority, which inevitably was based on a beginning, a founding in the past, with the Greek notion of transcending measurements and rules.'[28] The cumulative effect of the tradition – Greek philosophy, Roman law, and Christian faith – was such that 'general and transcendent standards under which the particular and immanent could be subsumed were now required for any political order.'[29] The combination of religious piety and respect for tradition is the corner-stone of the positive law tradition.

Totalitarianism, then, stands outside our political tradition because it does not invoke general and transcendent standards by which to gauge its laws: 'Totalitarian lawfulness, defying legality and pretending to establish the direct reign of justice on earth, executes the law of History or of Nature without translating it into standards of right and wrong for individual behaviour.'[30] The 'standard' of justice or authority instead becomes the extent to which the law of History or Nature can be actualized. Since totalitarian law is a law of immanent development, and not a spirit of founding or a principle of eternal justice, it is a law of movement rather than a stabilizing force in human affairs. With its ground in ideology, it seeks to alter the natures of men, not to stabilize them. The following passage from *The Origins* makes this point clear:

> When the Nazis talked about the law of nature or when the Bolsheviks talk about
> the law of history, neither nature or history is any longer the stabilizing source
> of authority for the actions of mortal men; they are movements in themselves.
> Underlying the Nazis' belief in race laws as the expression of the law of nature
> in man, is Darwin's idea of man as a product of a natural development which does
> not necessarily stop with the present species of human beings, just as under the
> Bolsheviks' belief in class struggle as the expression of the law of history lies
> Marx's notion of society as the product of a gigantic historical movement which
> races according to its own law of motion to the end of historical times when it will
> abolish itself.[31]

The disdain towards positive law manifested in the totalitarian state would not have been an effective weapon of domination were it not for the fact that people in the modern world had lost faith in the transcendent basis of justice. The move from a utilitarian political understanding, which holds that the meaning of acts and work-objects is located in their ability to sustain, not create, a human world, to a preoccupation with the activity of labour cannot be understood except in the context of modern atheism. As Arendt wrote in *The Human Condition*, the paradox of *homo faber* is that the things he makes are measured qualitatively by standards that lie outside his activity. Those standards need not be conceived as divine; indeed, Arendt thought it preferable that they not be divine, but rather something akin to the Roman spirit of founding. However, it is a fact that in the tradition as a whole the standard of positive law and the standards of work and thought have been conceived as the objects of philosophical contemplation or religious revelation. The loss of faith in the capacity of the mind to know justice, virtue, and truth in some essential sense is a major factor in the success of totalitarianism. The logic of ideology 'fills a vacuum' in the spiritual malaise of modern men, and hence is welcomed by them to a certain degree. As Arendt remarked: 'Totalitarian rulers rely on the compulsion with which we can compel ourselves.'[32]

Our traditional concepts of law were so bound up with religious experience that once men lost their fear of hell, their belief in the meting out of justice after death, they also lost any sense of legitimate political authority. This loss of the experience of faith makes all men in the Western world susceptible to the coercive power of ideology, and consequently open to the dangers of totalitarianism. Arendt cautioned that it was a basic weakness of humanist thought to presume that any nation can retain the tradition of Western thought without retaining religion as its motivating principle.[33] The two are mutually dependent. In so far as all Western men live in a world whose chief values are dictated by labour, and whose structure has lost the stability of 'ultimate standards,' all are open to the possibility of totalitarian ideology.

The establishment of a fictitious reality based on ideology and resistance to transcendence is only one dimension of totalitarianism. As I have tried to show, it is that dimension which is bound up with modern man's understanding. Ideology is successful in totalitarian states partly because of all the things whose absence Arendt lamented in *The Human Condition*: religious faith, the revelatory capacities of the senses, the intrinsic worth of the objects of work, and so on. These losses are common to all societies in modern Western civilization. Why then are not all Western men living under totalitarian domination?

Totalitarianism is a possibility for all modern civilization, but has actually occurred only in a limited context. The one outstanding characteristic of totalitarian states that separates them from any other modern state, be it liberal democratic or not, is the employment of terror. Thus we are back to the original premiss of this chapter: that terror is the essence of totalitarian government. The primary effect of terror is literally to eradicate the space between human beings, preventing them from communicating. Without terror the application of ideological rigour would be difficult, for every single individual in the state would have to be persuaded of the 'truth-claims' of the totalitarian government. Power based on an illegitimate construction of reality (that is, ideology) can only maintain itself with a network of terror. Totalitarian states typically have elaborate networks of terror and intimidation that are capable of subduing an entire population, including the elements of it that would otherwise resist the compelling persuasion of ideology.[34] Segments of the population may know vaguely about concentration camps, mysterious disappearances in the night, and arbitrary interrogations, but Arendt says that since they are prevented from communicating to others their suspicions and fears, this never-told information takes on the guise of fantasy: 'Inasmuch as man depends for his knowledge upon the affirmation and comprehension of his fellow men, this generally shared but individually guarded, this never-communicated information loses its quality of reality and assumes the nature of a mere nightmare.'[35]

Within the state itself, the reign of terror is imperative for maintaining power, but to ensure permanent control totalitarian regimes would have to extend their web of domination over the entire globe. Every bit of information, every intrusion of an outside reality from the non-totalitarian world, is a potential threat: 'The struggle for total domination of the total population of the earth, the elimination of every competing nontotalitarian reality, is inherent in the totalitarian regimes; if they do not pursue global rule as their ultimate goal they are only too likely to lose whatever power they have already seized.'[36] Effectively, the birth of every individual, and the potential for resistance that individuality holds, is a threat to totalitarian rule. Totalitarian states are, in effect, waging a war against the human race itself, a war that could come to an end only with the obliteration of humanity: 'Totalitarianism strives not toward despotic rule over men, but toward a system in which men are superfluous.'[37] This, for Arendt, is the greatest evil perpetrated by the totalitarian state. Ultimately, it aims to negate those very qualities – freedom and spontaneity – that make us human, and it attempts to do this by obliterating the space between human beings that is absolutely necessary for their emergence: terror 'destroys the one essential prerequisite of all freedom which is simply the capacity of motion which cannot exist without space.'[38]

We know from Arendt's thoughts on the human condition that she considered freedom of speech and action the definitive capacity of human beings. It is even constitutive of thought. She wrote at the end of The Human Condition that thought is possible wherever men live under the conditions of political freedom.[39] This is emphasized even more in her essay entitled 'What Is Freedom?' in which she wrote: 'Without a politically guaranteed public realm, freedom lacks the worldly space to make its appearance. To be sure it may still dwell in men's hearts as desire or will or hope or yearning; but the human heart, as we all know, is a very dark place, and whatever goes on in its obscurity can hardly be called a demonstrable fact. Freedom as a demonstrable fact and politics coincide and are related to each another like two sides of the same matter.'[40] This brings us to a fundamental question: Does the preservation of freedom in a constitutionally protected public realm somehow immunize communities from the threat of totalitarianism? To what extent is democracy, with its attendant qualities of free speech, toleration, and public assembly, an antidote to the totalitarian world? There is a sense in which Arendt thought that liberal democracy in some form could perform this task, and she certainly had much to say about non-totalitarian political formations, with which we shall deal shortly.

The question as to whether democratic political institutions can in themselves protect freedom was most directly addressed in an exchange between Eric Voegelin and Hannah Arendt that came about as a consequence of Voegelin's review essay of *The Origins of Totalitarianism*.[41] The review was taken very seriously by Arendt and she acknowledged that Voegelin had raised some fundamental philosophical issues.[42] Voegelin's main criticism was that Arendt failed to establish clearly whether totalitarianism as a political phenomenon is simply an extreme manifestation of the gnostic 'syndrome' of the modern world (hence being part of the entire ideological, secular strain of modern politics) or whether it is qualitatively different from other ideological systems such as liberal democratic ones. Voegelin was very clear about his own point of view. Totalitarian states and liberal states are symptomatic of the same spiritual derailment: 'The essential immanentism which unites them overrides the differences of ethos which separate them.'[43] He objected to Arendt's claim that human nature is at stake in the twentieth century, saying that: 'A "nature" cannot be changed or transformed; a "change of nature" is a contradiction of terms.'[44] Voegelin believed that there is such a thing as human nature, that it is a permanent capacity of man, and that it can be 'discovered' in any time or any period, no matter what the political conditions might be. Arendt's 'nightmarish fright' he attributed to her being 'impressed by the imbecile' who mistakes immanent historical events for essences.[45] To Voegelin the potentialities of response to any given situation (even in the extreme situation of totalitarianism) are rooted in the potentialities of the individual soul, and not in any specific political configuration. In short, totalitarianism cannot 'eradicate' human nature, and neither can any democratic institutionalization of freedom and public space produce it.

Arendt's response was quick and short: 'I proceed from facts and events instead of intellectual affinities and influences.'[46] The facts, according to her, are that liberals are not totalitarians. Though both may be afflicted by certain ideological falsehoods, it is *not* their shared commitment to ideology that is the most important element. To identify the ideological element, or 'immanent sectarianism' as Voegelin called it, as the single most important element of totalitarian and liberal states is to obscure the very real difference between living in a free world and living under the conditions of interrogation, torture, and imprisonment. Terror, more than ideology, for Arendt, demarcated the uniqueness of totalitarianism, although, as we have seen, she certainly agreed with Voegelin that ideological thinking played a prominent role. But ideology for Arendt becomes truly dangerous only when it ceases to be the motivation for a political movement, and becomes the official dogma of the state. It is at this juncture that terror is introduced to obliterate all alternative modes of thinking. Terror has the potential to accomplish this end by effectively cutting off the free flow of ideas between people. She feared that the abrogation of 'space' between human beings over a sustained period of time would alter human capacities for action and thought *because* the experience of freedom would be extinguished from the experience of being alive. 'Historically,' she wrote, 'we know of man's nature only insofar as it has existence, and no realm of eternal essences will ever console us if man loses his essential capacities.'[47] Out of Arendt's analysis of totalitarianism in general and her reply to Voegelin in particular emerges an even stronger commitment to politics as the guarantee of human freedom. Her work on totalitarianism faithfully reaffirms the central focus of *The Human Condition*: the world of appearances.

New Beginnings: Revolution and Democracy

If the appearance of totalitarianism in the twentieth century seemed to Arendt to be one of the blackest moments of Western history, there were other political 'appearances' in the same century that heartened her. She saw the potentiality for freedom in various revolutionary movements, in the student uprisings of the 1960s, and in the town council meetings of New England. Since she emphasized how important action, public 'space,' and freedom were for preserving certain human capacities, one would expect that these positive political trends would have been regarded by Arendt as a remedy for the dangers of totalitarianism.

There has been much debate about whether Arendt was a democrat; whether she saw democratic institutions as an adequate antidote to totalitarianism. We find disparate judgments on this issue. George Kateb, for example, sees Arendt as a champion of direct democracy (though neglectful of the strength of representative democracy).[48] On the same subject – Arendt and democracy – Sheldon Wolin has written that Arendt was anti-democratic. He argues that Arendt's strongest influence in her writings on political action, notably *On Revolution*, was de Tocqueville, and that she shared with him a fear of democratic politics.[49] That there can be such contradictory views of Arendt's ideas on politics ought to tell us something about the ambiguity of Arendt's position. In fact, she wrote no systematic work on democracy as such; rather, there exists a selection of articles on such wide-ranging topics as the 1956 Hungarian Revolution, the founding of the American republic, Roman *humanitas*, and a laudatory biographical sketch of Rosa Luxemburg. All of these pieced together give us some idea of what Arendt's vision of non-totalitarian politics was. If she was a democrat, she certainly was not a conventional one; but that is not the real issue. What we want to know is if Arendt sustained her notion that certain kinds of action furnish the proper 'space' for political freedom. We want to do two things: (1) establish in what kinds of political action Arendt thought freedom of action could be realized; and (2) establish if these political institutions could provide an adequate response to totalitarianism.

We have a sense of what Arendt thought the public space should be from *The Human Condition*. It was a 'space' populated by peers, by human beings whose intersubjectivity constituted a pluralistic community. It was a 'space' into which the repetitive activity of the 'labourer' and the single-minded purposiveness of the 'worker' do not enter. Action conducted in its best sense achieves its own end in the creative process of exchange among speaking beings. Its outcome is unpredictable because it has no sought-after end other than the disclosure of the real being of the people who participate. As Sheldon Wolin summarized Arendt's portrayal of the political realm in *The Human Condition*: 'It signified not a state or a society but a determinate public space, a forum, an agora, set aside, jealously defended so that those men who wished to test themselves by the highest standards of excellence might compete, by speech and action, in the presence of their peers. It was to be a politics of lofty ambition, glory and honor.'[50]

This description of the public 'space' in *The Human Condition* is most often equated by Arendt with the ancient Greek *polis*, but in other writings she evoked a similar picture of politics in radically different settings.[51] She wrote passionately about modern revolutions and their promise of furnishing a new 'agora' for the disclosure of the 'who.' *On Revolution*, arguably Arendt's most popular book, defends revolutions as 'the only political events which confront us directly and inevitably with the problem of beginning.'[52] The glorious aspect of revolution, for Arendt, was its close bond with 'natality,' its effort to make a radically free, new beginning in human association. But her idea of revolution has little in common with other contemporary notions in that she did not view revolution, in the best sense, as any kind of fight against oppression or liberation from exploitation. For her, revolutions are legitimate only if they approximate the ideal of human freedom achieved in the ancient agora: the establishment of a peerage among equals for the sheer enjoyment of freedom. For this end Arendt was willing to pay the price of a violent beginning.[53] Revolutions, then, are defined as follows: 'Only when change occurs in the sense of a new beginning, where violence is used to constitute an altogether different form of government, to bring about the formation of a new body politic, where the liberation from oppression aims at least at the constitution of freedom can we speak of revolution.'[54]

Revolutions defeat their purpose – the new beginning – when they get bogged down with the idea of liberation from some form or agent of oppression, for in this respect the revolution is enacted only against something – liberation is always *from* something specific – but does not hold any vision for the future. Arendt cited the French Revolution as the classic case of a potential revolution that forfeited its 'new beginning' in the fight against poverty and misery. When attention was shifted from creating a new space for freedom to liberating the many from their collective misery, the opportunity to fashion new institutions and channels for the exchange of opinions was lost: 'The Revolution, when it turned from the foundation of freedom to the liberation of man from suffering, broke down the barriers of endurance and liberated, as it were, the devastating forces of misfortune and misery instead.'[55] There are echoes here of Arendt's distinctions among labour, work, and action. It is as though she were saying that once the concerns of the downtrodden and poor, in short the masses, are allowed to dominate the political realm, the potential for true action is sacrificed. In contrast to what Arendt regarded as a legitimate plurality – a plenitude of voices expressing many informed and diverse opinions – the masses are ill-equipped for public action precisely because the common nature of their plight overwhelms any differencne or 'plurality' among them: 'The political trouble which misery of the people holds in store is that manyness can in fact assume the guise of oneness.'[56] The solidarity of the unfortunate, said Arendt, can never be converted into a viable basis for political action. Whenever the concerns of the social take over the concerns of the political – that is, whenever the needs of the body are stronger than the desire for freedom – the consequence is likely to be a reign of terror, the only solution to the unruly and passionate violence of the masses.[57]

Compared to the French Revolution, which failed to create a public space to provide for freedom, Arendt thought the American Revolution was an outstanding success. In large part she thought its success could be attributed to the abundance of the New World, which allowed Americans a measure of relief from the burdens of poverty. Americans did not suffer from the poverty and misery that had figured so prominently in the revolutionary base in France: 'They were not driven by want, and the revolution was not overwhelmed by them.'[58] For this reason, she said, their concerns were political rather than social.

Arendt's understanding of the American Revolution was in some respects incredibly naïve. She claimed that among the principles shared by the men of the American Revolution was that 'a republic was constituted by an exchange of opinion between equals.'[59] As one reviewer commented: 'Despite Hannah Arendt's strong implication of the absence in America of the kinds of social discontents so evident first in France and a century later in Russia, all evidence suggests the discontents were present in America, even if in more moderate degree, and were the fuel of the social revolution that took place in this country.'[60] It is not the immediate task here to determine the accuracy of Arendt's interpretation of the American Revolution; we are interested in how her idiosyncratic view of American politics sheds light on her broader view of politics. The American Revolution came as close as any modern political event to her understanding of what political action ought to be.

The Founding Fathers, said Arendt, consciously set out to create a public domain for the voicing of opinions; they were concerned with the preservation of public life as the embodiment of freedom. Arendt made much of the notion of 'public happiness,' saying that 'the Americans knew that public freedom consisted in having a share in public business, and that the activities connected with this business by no means constituted a burden but gave those who discharged them in public a feeling of happiness they could acquire nowhere else.'[61] Arendt claimed that the notion that happiness can be fulfilled only by acting in a public sphere, exchanging opinions with one's equals, is unequalled anywhere else in the modern history of revolutions. She cited a passage from Jefferson in which he expressed the hope that he would meet in Congress after death with his peers and his ancient colleagues – presumably the Greeks and Romans. In this remark of Jefferson's, Arendt said, 'we have the candid admission that life in Congress, the joys of discourse, of legislation, of transacting business, of persuading and being persuaded, were to Jefferson no less conclusively a foretaste of an eternal bliss to come than the delights of contemplation had been for medieval piety.'[62] The achievement of the Founding Fathers was that they sought revolution not for the sake of realizing any determinate end such as a just or equal society, but for the purpose of simply creating an open-ended public forum.

What would Arendt's ideal republic look like? It would be an association among peers, but it would necessarily exclude all those whose talents and time for public display were not up to the standards of eloquent and dispassionate discourse: 'Freedom in a positive sense is possible only among equals, and equality itself is by no means a universally valid principle.'[63] She stated that the 'political passions' – that is, courage, the pursuit of public happiness, the taste of public freedom – are extraordinary under all circumstances.[64] Arendt's vision of the prospects for the realization of public happiness was to create spaces 'to which the people at large would have entrance and from which an elite could be selected, or rather, where it could select itself.'[65] She seemed to have faith that if these spaces were created and nurtured, that is, kept separate from the social concerns of the body politic, the principle of self-selection would really work. Arendt envisioned that this could be possible in a council democracy, where grass-roots organizations would elect 'those few from all walks of life who have a taste for political freedom and cannot be happy without it. Politically, they are the best and it is the task of good government and the sign of a well-ordered republic to assure them of their rightful place in the public realm.'[66]

Arendt's view of the ideal republic, then, can hardly be called democratic in the sense that the term usually conveys. She thought that universal suffrage could be done away with, without much grievous effect. From her point of view, general suffrage had never performed the task of extending political participation to the many. People do not participate in politics in so-called democratic states any more than they do in autocratic ones. All that has resulted from universal suffrage is that politics has become a career for the ambitious, the wealthy, and the socially advantaged.[67] Furthermore, these elites are elected into office by the masses, who have neither an informed opinion nor even a genuine interest in politics. The kind of elite that Arendt favoured would represent the best 'political' beings in the society by giving them proper channels of access to power. 'Only those who as voluntary members of an "elementary republic" have demonstrated that they care for more than their private happiness and are concerned about the state of the world would have the right to be heard.'[68]

To reiterate, Arendt thought that freedom was possible only among equals, and that political equality could never be extended universally. The demands of the social realm are such that it would be impossible for all human beings to experience the kind of happiness she associated with political action. Arendt's perspective on the ideal polity is borne out in other writings besides *On Revolution*. In reflections on the 1956 Hungarian Revolution Arendt spoke of the glory of the uprising 'for the sake of freedom and hardly anything else,' and of the intgegrity of the council representatives who had been selected for their 'personal integrity, courage and judgment.'[69] The revolution's initial successes she attributed to the fact that it was triggered by the love of freedom, not by any overwhelming social concerns like hunger or deprivation: 'Their [the revolutionaries'] motive was neither their own nor their fellow-citizens' material misery, but exclusively freedom and truth.'[70] The revolution in Hungary also held a special significance for Arendt because of the kind of representative institutions it adopted; councils from all walks of life, among intellectuals, workers, and artists, sent elected representatives to put forth their views in higher councils. What impressed Arendt was precisely the lack of organized channels of representation, the absence of a party machine. The council system, as opposed to party politics, was what Arendt regarded as 'true democracy.'[71] The Hungarian Revolution, then, stood as a twentieth-century example of the kind of politics Arendt imagined must have been engaged in at the time of the American Revolution. It also carried for her the message of Rosa Luxemburg, someone whom Arendt greatly admired. The spontaneity and apparently anarchic nature of the Hungarian Revolution seemed to be concrete 'proof' of Rosa Luxemburg's notion that ' "good organization does not precede action but is the product of it," that "the organization of revolutionary action can and must be learnt in revolution itself, as one can only learn swimming in the water," that revolutions are "made" by nobody and break out "spontaneously," and that "the pressure for action" always comes "from below." '[72]

What the American Revolution, the Hungarian Revolution, and the Russian October Revolution had in common, apart from their 'spontaneity,' their 'grass-roots' base, and their inspired leadership, was their conspicuous failure to live up to the promise of freedom. In the case of the American Revolution Arendt felt that the desire for wealth and material well-being took over and ultimately subverted the goal of 'public happinerss.' That is, the vision of public happiness was replaced by the goal of liberty to pursue one's own private interests with a minimum of interference by the state. Arendt summed up this transition by saying: 'This transformation corresponds with great precision to the invasion of the public realm by society; it is as though the originally politically values were translated into social values.'[73]

In the case of the twentieth-century revolutions, the most conspicuous failure has been the inability of the revolutionary spirit to sustain itself when faced with the actual administration of the state: 'The fatal mistake of the councils has always been that they themselves did not distinguish clearly between participation in public affairs and administration or management of things in the public interest.'[74] Again, these are intimations that the failure was partly due to a shift of attention from the purely political to administrative matters. When 'men of action and freedom' turn their talents to management and what Arendt disdainfully called in *The Human Condition* 'housekeeping tasks,' the public-spiritedness of their cause seems inevitably to degenerate into oligarchic and bureaucratic functioning.

Though Arendt exalted revolution as the only way to make 'new beginnings' in the modern world, and though she favoured, in theory, something like council-democracy, led by a 'self-appointed' elite, there is little indication in any of her works that she thought this kind of political formation was a viable, practical possibility. She was encouraged by the student movement of the 1960s, particularly by the shape it took in the United States with its emphasis on civil rights, but she feared that it would be 'eaten away by fanaticism, ideologies and a destructiveness that often borders on the criminal on one side, by boredom on the other.'[75] She seemed at times to be uplifted by the tradition of civil disobedience in the United States. She saw the possibility for incorporating the spirit of revolutionary change in institutional mechanisms that would provide for civil disobedience as an integral part of the political system. On the road to a recovery of the public-spiritedness of the American founding, the 'first step,' she said, 'would be to obtain the same recognition for the civil-disobedient minorities that is accorded the numerous special-interest groups.'[76] She once remarked that she saw in the council system 'the possibility of forming a new concept of the state,' but in the same breath she admitted: 'If you ask me now what prospect it has of being realized, then I must say to you: Very slight, if at all.'[77]

We can say then that Arendt did have a fairly coherent idea of what a 'good' polity would look like. It was not a democratic state, but one in which a self-appointed elite would exercise freedom of action. Arendt never spoke in more detail about the precise workings of such a state. As her friend Hans Morgenthau wrote of her views on revolution and politics: 'There is a romantic element in Hannah Arendt's conception of freedom and of the mechanism by which it is to be accomplished. For she tells us nothing about how freedom is to be preserved, how it is to be guarded against the enemies within.'[78] She tells us what is glorious about the revolutionary spirit, but she could not recall one single instance in which a revolution fulfilled its goal of creating a space for freedom. We have to conclude, then, that revolution, or a 'revolutionary council-democracy' as she understood it, cannot guarantee that freedom will be preserved. All revolutions are overpowered by social conditions that limit their success, by organizational problems, and by the private ambitions of administrative types who end up wielding power. When revolutions fail, in fact, they end up producing the very opposite of the free community that they promised. They can end up in totalitarian forms of rule, for example, as happened in the case of the Russian Revolution. Arendt was aware of the precarious balance upon which all revolutions rest. As one of her more admiring critics said: 'No one has ever had a keener sense – a Burkean, Tocquevillean, Michelsian sense – of the monotonous regularity with which revolutions generated in the name of the people and freedom so quickly become machines of despotism than Hannah Arendt.'[79]

There was an intensely pessimistic side to Arendt, as we have already seen in her reflections in *The Human Condition*, but her gloomy predictions about the possibility for political action are clearer in her essay 'The Crisis in Culture.' We find here the same laments about mass society, about a world that has been overtaken by the concerns of the *animal laborans*. Arendt felt that any vestiges of culture – by which she meant the admiration of things in themselves and the participation in politics for the sheer enjoyment of exchange with one's peers – had been swept away by philistines who pursued all things only for their own self-aggrandizement: 'A consumer's society cannot possibly know how to take care of a world and the things that belong exclusively to the space of worldly appearances because its central attitude toward all objects, the attitude of consumption, spells ruin to everything it touches.'[80] The chances for a restoration of culture and freedom in the so-called free world, then, were negligible according to Arendt. The chances are even slimmer in the Communist bloc, where ideology and police control impose much more visible and physical blockages on the freedom of action. Arendt saw absolutely no hope for the catharsis of revolution to have any effect there: 'It certainly would be rather unwise to expect from the Russian people, after forty years of tyranny and thirty years of totalitarianism, the same spirit and the same political productivity which the Hungarian people showed in their most glorious hour.'[81]

In sum, Arendt did not hope for much in the way of institutional change that could serve as a practical antidote to the ever-threatening presence of totalitarianism. Where the channels of communication are not forcibly repressed by the state, as they are in the Soviet Union, they are still blocked by the prejudices and inclinations of modern mass society. Arendt seemed to have reached a dead end with her 'politics of action.'

The Failure of Action

We can conclude that Arendt thought that freedom and action could be realized, even ideally, only in small peer groups of a political elite composed of human beings truly dedicated to the disclosing aspect of public life. She was not a democrat and did not advocate universal suffrage. We can also conclude that she did not think that political action could provide any realistic buffer against the tendencies towards totalitarianism. She did not theorize about any institutional remedy for totalitarianism.[82]

Many of her critics thought Arendt was far too pessimistic in her judgment about the failure of political action (specifically the republican tradition) in the modern period. Stephen Whitfield, in his study of Arendt's theory of totalitarianism, wrote: 'What one misses in Arendt's thought, for all its subtlety, originality and immediacy, is a fuller appreciation of liberalism as a force inherently hostile to totalitarianism. For as a set of political principles, not as an ideology masking particular economic interests, liberalism has been the most effective historical foe of total domination.'[83] Whitfield's praise of liberalism can be dismissed fairly easily in light of Arendt's own analysis of the historical genesis of totalitarianism. Liberals are not totalitarians, as she informed Eric Voegelin, and as she would no doubt agree with Whitfield, but certain traditions of a liberal society, including the preoccupation with privacy and the protection of property, threaten to override what Arendt regarded as the positive liberal tradition of toleration and freedom of association. She stated that there was no way in which we could say for sure that liberal democracy would remain faithful to the spirit of freedom. It is true, she conceded, that the revolutionary ideas of public happiness and political freedom have never left American politics altogether, but she was undecided about the future of 'freedom' in American constitutional democracy: 'Whether this structure has a granite groundwork capable of withstanding the futile antics of a society intent upon affluence and consumption ... only the future can tell. There exist today as many signs to justify hope as there are to instil fear.'[84]

There are other democratic critics who also disagree with Arendt's pessimism, but who do not share Stephen Whitfield's faith in the present structure of American politics. Jürgen Habermas in fact shares Arendt's fear of the 'privations' of modern societies and feels that one of her most valuable insights was into the connection between mass democracy – comprising alienated and dispossessed individuals – and totalitarianism. However, her idea of an 'ideal' state, according to Habermas, was almost too näive to be taken seriously. What she wanted was 'a state which is relieved of the administrative processing of social problems; a politics which is cleansed of socio-economic issues; an institutionalization of public liberty which is independent of the organization of public wealth; a radical democracy which inhibits its liberating efficacy just at the boundaries where political oppression ceases and social repression begins.'[85]

The idea that politics can be completely divorced from social concerns is unfathomable in the context of the modern state. Habermas suggested that the remedy for mass alienation and privatism was not to separate out public-spirited individuals from privatistic ones and secure the former a place in power, but rather to alter the conditions of modern social stratification so that political participation is a viable alternative for more people. The prohibitions against public freedom, to Habermas, are structural ones; they make it impossible for anyone to exercise autonomy or freedom of action – even those clear-headed and free-thinking individuals who Arendt thought could constitute a 'political peer group.' According to Habermas, Arendt underestimated the extent to which institutions and systems in a complex technological world militate against any kind of freedom.[86] The 'unimpaired intersubjectivity' that she longed for was doomed to fail within her own analysis of the tasks of revolutionary change, since Arendt did not analyse sufficiently the mechanisms of control in a modern society.

Sheldon Wolin also shares Arendt's position on the alienating, unpolitical nature of modern society. He, like Habermas, thinks that much more all-encompassing change would be necessary to restore freedom to the public realm; but he is more optimistic than Habermas that this restoration can be achieved. For Wolin, the 'solution' to the problem of mass society lies not in the separation of the social and political realms, but rather in the recognition of their interdependence: 'The problem of the political is not to clear a space from which society is to be kept out but it is rather to ground power in commonality while reverencing diversity.'[87] To claim, as Arendt did, that the majority of the people are incapable in any way of determining what the end of politics ought to be may be an 'intellectual conceit,' Wolin argued, that is bred from the resentment felt by the intellectual when he experiences his own displacement in a capitalist society.[88] Wolin claims that Arendt, in all her works, ignored two of the most essential concerns of politics: power and justice. She has no way of accounting for justice except to believe that in a truly free society the best and the worst could find their proper place in the polity; and her definition of power is so narrowly conceived that it cannot account for the structural blockages of the modern state.

Here Wolin emphasizes the same point as Habermas. Specifically, Arendt did not seem to understand the characteristic unique to the modern state: it can generate surplus power, that is, a power greater than the co-operation and reciprocity of citizens can possibly create. For Wolin, it is this surplus power, and not the existential conversion of citizens to the mentality of the animal laborans, that has led to the massive depoliticization of modern society: 'Surplus ... becomes the province of administration; it is managed and administered in the form of programs, including programs for the development of power converted into weapons and man power. In all of this, the political, which had emerged as shared concerns and involvements, has disappeared.'[89] For Wolin, the only way to break the back of the modern state, along with its attendant features of arms build-up, administrative apparatus, and bureaucracy, is through massive democratic participation on the part of those who are most disadvantaged.

Arendt did not believe that any form of structural change could alter modern political conditions. Though her critics have accused her, often justifiably, of being overly romantic, elitist, and naïve in her considerations about the ideal council-democracy, Arendt did not think her ideal council system would, or could, come into existence. Her analysis of the modern malaise, its historical precedents, and its dominant mode of thinking was too complex for her to entertain so simple a solution. She glorified the political, but only as a space that remained tied to specific, individual action. In this respect, Wolin is right in saying that for Arendt 'politics was essentially dramaturgic.'[90] She was distinctively un-modern in her refusal to analyse politics in terms of movements, interests, classes, and so on. She always brought any discussion of politics back to the specific character of the individuals who practised politics. Ultimately, she could see no structural resolution to modern problems; structure of any type to her obscured the reality of living, speaking, diverse human beings by slotting them into 'categories' for the convenience of social scientists. The idea that a specific class, or a specific ideology, or any similar reductive category could hold the key to real reform did not make sense to her because all such terms are abstractions that combine the diverse tendencies of the individuals whom they are supposed to identify in a predetermined fashion.

In an open forum discussion at York University, Toronto, in 1974 Arendt was asked why she had not given more of her attention to the concrete problems of modern society, that is, to the 'questions of class, the question of property.' Arendt replied that she thought such terms had no 'disclosing quality,' that is, that they do not describe the real constellations of the modern world. For example, she thought class was a confusing abstraction that no longer describes the real divisions of power in the twentieth century.[91] She rejected all formulas for political change because they ignore the unpredictable and spontaneous input of individuals, who are more than simply members of a class, a nation, or any such category. Arendt's appreciation of the capabilities of people to prove themselves exceptions to any theory is demonstrated quaintly in a remark she once made: 'The trend of a white wall is to get dirty with time, unless someone appears and redecorates the room.'[92] Similarly, there may be 'trends' towards class warfare, bureaucratization, totalitarianism, or whatever, but the unpredictability and imaginativeness of human beings are such that these trends are not determinate. The patterns are made and broken by human beings. They do not have a life of their own.

Because of her faith in the potential integrity and spontaneity of individual action, Arendt did not share the views of her critics – Habermas and Wolin – that the perception of patterns and structures in modern society is the key to a transformation of modern politics. Rather, she was interested in why individuals do, or do not, resist the world around them, and in the diverse manners in which they do so. Even though she realized that the modern conditions of bureaucracy, technology, and social stratification make it difficult for people to actively engage in, or even think about, change, she thought that the independence of the human spirit did not make it impossible. When she looked over the major events of the twentieth century, its encouraging 'beginnings' and its devastating forms of tyranny, she was struck not only by the failures on a grand scale, but also by the brilliant flashes of individual thought and action that defied the bleak pessimism of those who believe that structures prohibit independence. Arendt's book *Men in Dark Times* is an assembly of such unique individuals, and she wrote in its preface: 'That even in the darkest of times we have the right to expect some illumination, and that such illumination may well come less from theories and concepts than from the uncertain, flickering and often weak light that some men and women, in their lives and their works, will kindle under almost all circumstances and shed over the time span that was given them on earth – this conviction is the inarticulate background against which these profiles were drawn.'[93]

In *Men in Dark Times* Arendt turned her attention away from the question 'why does politics fail?' and towards the question 'why do individuals succeed?' Here, in these scattered essays on diverse people, she began her exploration of the psyche of the individual. These biographical sketches are a prelude to what would occupy Arendt throughout her later years: the life of the mind. It seems that in her earlier works she had tried to balance two sorts of loyalties: one to politics and collective action, and the other to the imaginative thinker. Though she is best known for her earlier writings on politics, there is no question that she abandoned this loyalty to pursue an inquiry into the nature of independent thought. Arendt herself dated the shift with her report on the trial of Adolf Eichmann in Jerusalem. Observing Eichmann, Arendt concluded that his most outstanding feature was that he did not think. She asked herself whether the crime of genocide by means of the organization of concentration camps attributed to Eichmann might be the result of his inability to think.[94] It was this question that led to the central task of Arendt's last work, *The Life of the Mind*, in which she asked: 'Could the activity of thinking as such, the habit of examining whatever happens to come to pass or to attract attention, regardless of results and specific content, could this activity be among the conditions that make men abstain from evil-doing or even actually "condition" them against it?'[95]

Beginning with her report on the Eichmann trial, Arendt gave up trying to find a 'political solution' to the totalitarian threat of the twentieth century. The compilation of factors in the complex structure of modern society seemed to her too formidable to even attempt a theory along such lines. Instead, she tried simply to understand what motivates those rare individuals who, in dark times, do think and act independently and justly; and conversely, in the case of Eichmann, what motivates those who are swept up unthinkingly in mass movements and criminal behaviour. The following chapter will trace this fundamental shift of focus in Arendt's concerns.

3 The Problem of Evil

Observations on Eichmann

Arendt undertook a reconsideration of the relationship between thought and action, prompted by her observations on Nazi war criminal Adolf Eichmann, whose trial was held in Jerusalem in 1961. Arendt's account of the trial was published first as a series of articles in the *New Yorker* and later as a book entitled *Eichmann in Jerusalem: A Report on the Banality of Evil*. Her account provoked considerable controversy, partly because of her own interpretation of the meaning of the trial, but also because of the inherent sensitivity of the issues it raised. The trial of Eichmann – the man who was the 'real engineer of the Final Solution' for the extermination of the Jews in Nazi Germany – served as a forum from which the memories of the Holocaust could sound a voice to the world. In some respects, according to Arendt, it was intended to demonstrate that 'only in Israel could a Jew be safe and live an honorable life.'[1] Then there were the particular circumstances of the trial: Eichmann had been kidnapped by the Israelis from his home in Argentina and brought to Jerusalem where he was to be tried by a retroactive law in a court of the victors. Arendt tried, in her account, to assess all these factors and to answer various questions: Was the trial legal? Was justice done in the final verdict of the court? Did the trial really come to terms with the specific nature of Eichmann's crimes?

Her answers to these questions were complex, but one main thread of argument runs through the book, and that is that the Israeli judicial system failed to understand the nature of crime in a totalitarian state and, therefore, did not really succeed in understanding Eichmann. This does not mean that Eichmann should have been set free or that the court failed to establish his guilt. Arendt states unequivocally that the arguments advanced by some against the legitimacy of the trial, based on quibblings over the legal authority of the Israeli court and the illegality of kidnapping, showed a preoccupation with formality that only obfuscated the fundamental issues. It was right that Eichmann should have been tried and condemned by Jews, his principal victims, but Arendt thought that the magnitude of his crimes warranted trial by the entire human race. For this reason, 'insofar as the victims were Jews, it was right and proper that a Jewish court should sit in judgment; but insofar as the crime was a crime against humanity, it needed an international tribunal.'[2] The crime of genocide requires that all human beings inquire into the nature of justice, the limits of action, and the quality of life in the twentieth century. Since Arendt regarded totalitarianism as a radically new political phenomenon involving unprecedented forms of action and criminality, it demanded justice of a different sort than that which a traditional court could provide. The Israeli court failed, then, because it did not understand the novelty of Eichmann's crimes, or the novelty of the political context in which they were committed. Arendt had hoped that the trial would serve as an opportunity to confront the uniqueness of totalitarianism, and thus to produce some guidelines for avoiding a similar catastrophe in the future. This it did not do. Arendt concluded her assessment of the trial by saying: 'I think it is safe to predict that this last of the Successor trials will no more, and perhaps even less than its predecessors, serve as a valid precedent for future trials of such crimes. This might be of little import in view of the fact that its main purpose – to prosecute and to defend, to judge and to punish Adolf Eichmann – was achieved, if it were not for the rather uncomfortable but hardly deniable possibility that similar crimes may be committed in the future.'[3]

Arendt viewed the trial and the evidence brought forth in it in the context of her more general concerns about totalitarianism. Her recounting of the proceedings of the trial was interspersed with comments on the behaviour of aggressors and victims in the Nazi state. She claimed, for example, that the passivity of the Jews as a whole and the collaboration of Jewish functionaries with the Nazis in some instances 'offers the most striking insight into the totality of the moral collapse the Nazis caused in respectable European society – not only in Germany, but in almost all countries, not only among the persecutors but also among the victims.'[4] She also spoke of the futility of 'inner emigration' in the face of political catastrophe.[5] These and other critical remarks can be traced to Arendt's conviction that totalitarian crimes are not the isolated acts of a nation gone berserk, but evidence of a total collapse of all standards of behaviour in the modern Western world. The general preponderance of ideological thinking, the 'retreat' to private life, and the denigration of the world of things, all are held to account for this collapse, in the midst of which neither assailant nor victim knew what was the proper course of action, and in which Eichmann was just one example of what human beings are capable of doing under such conditions.

Arendt's emphasis on the far-reaching effects of totalitarianism was misinter-preted by some critics as a method of pardoning Eichmann and extending part of the blame for his actions to his victims. One commentator said that Arendt seemed to have a peculiar repugnance towards those who did not act to save their own lives under the duress of terror and the threat of imminent death.[6] Another wrote that for Arendt 'to kill millions is banal; any one of us could do it under the pressure of a totalitarian state. But to be among the sufferers is somehow culpable.'[7] Perhaps the most scathing rebuke came from Gershom Scholem, Arendt's long-time friend and a leading Jewish scholar, who regarded Arendt's tone as 'flippant' and said that her account of the trial left him with feelings of 'shame' and 'bitterness' towards its author.[8]

These reactions caused Arendt no small amount of distress. Apart from the fact that she felt she had been misunderstood, she was, by all accounts, grieved by the viciousness with which what she called the 'Jewish "establishment" in Israel and America' had cast her out as a betrayer of her own people.[9] Elisabeth Young-Bruehl reports that, following the Eichmann controversy, 'hostility surrounded her wherever she went.'[10]

I believe that these criticisms were, for the most part, unfounded. It is true that Arendt had tried to make sense of Eichmann in the context of her earlier thoughts about totalitarianism, but she made it perfectly clear to the attentive reader that she deplored any effort to exonerate Eichmann of his personal responsibility. She was especially opposed to the suggestion that 'there is an Eichmann in every one of us.' Such abstractions from the particular crime and the particular individual only obscure the distinctions between just and unjust action, as she made clear in the following passage: 'It can be held that the issue is no longer a particular human being, a single distinct individual in the dock, but rather the German people in general, or anti-Semitism in all its forms, or the whole of modern history, or the nature of man and original sin – so that ultimately, the entire human race sits invisibly beside the defendant in the dock ... I need scarcely say that I would never have gone to Jerusalem if I had shared these views.'[11]

Inasmuch as courts try individuals for their actions, the Israelis could not go beyond establishing guilt or innocence in Eichmann's case. This the court did, and Arendt did not dispute the verdict. Her major concern was that the consensus on which the authority of courts is based in the first place – the pre-legal understanding of what constitutes criminality – was inadequate to deal with the case. The real controversy, in her view, was not about the guilt of Eichmann versus the 'guilt' of the Jews in complying with genocide. The language of guilt and innocence has no place in such questions. The controversy surrounds our ability, or lack thereof, to understand the qualitative difference between the crimes of the totalitarian world and those of the non-totalitarian world. Eichmann's banality was a most terrifying thing to Arendt because it signified that he was incapable of independent, critical thought. This incapacity did not make Eichmann innocent in the eyes of the law. What Arendt discovered at the trial was that lack of thought can produce more disaster for mankind than evil intent: 'That such remoteness from reality and such thoughtlessness can wreak more havoc than all the evil instincts taken together which, perhaps, are inherent in man – that was, in fact, the lesson one could learn in Jerusalem. But it was a lesson, neither an explanation of the phenomenon nor a theory about it.'[12]

The lesson, as it turns out, had a profound effect on Arendt's own thinking. It is curious that she so adamantly defended Eichmann's individual responsibility, given what she wrote on the subject of totalitarianism. Many of Arendt's critics, who charged that she was exonerating Eichmann of his personal guilt, may well have been reading into the trial account some of her conclusions in *The Origins of Totalitarianism*. If we were to extrapolate the latter and apply them to Eichmann's case it would be difficult indeed to establish his responsibility for his acts. Arendt had said that totalitarianism made it hard, if not impossible, for men living under its domination to think or act independently. When her critics – notably Eric Voegelin – had pushed her on this point, she had responded that man's traditional capacities for free thought and action were historical, not essential ones.

Now, in 1963, Arendt expected Eichmann as a human being to be able to exercise these traditional capacities, even though he lived in a totalitarian 'world.' She did not accept that ignorance or insanity or passive obedience to political authority in a totalitarian state should even be considered as possible defences of Eichmann's actions. Any of these might offer an explanation of why Eichmann did what he did but, according to Arendt, none of them could relieve him of his personal guilt. The fact that Eichmann committed a crime that 'offends nature' was, for Arendt, sufficient reason for his condemnation. In other words, she did not think that *intentionality* had to be proved in order to establish Eichmann's guilt. She made it absolutely clear where she stood on this issue: the difference between just and unjust action does not depend upon the subjective intentions of an actor. Justice and injustice are in some sense absolute categories that retain their universal validity no matter how many people fail to recognize them. The following statement in the epilogue to *Eichmann in Jerusalem* indicates that Arendt thought that Eichmann's crimes offended 'nature' itself.

> Foremost among the larger issues at stake in the Eichmann trial was the assumption current in all modern legal systems that intent to do wrong is necessary for the commission of a crime. On nothing, perhaps, has civilized jurisprudence prided itself more than on this taking into account of the subjective factor. Where this intent is absent, where, for whatever reasons, even reasons of moral insanity, the

ability to distinguish between right and wrong is impaired, we feel no crime has been committed. We refuse, and consider as barbaric, the propositions that 'a great crime offends nature, so that the very earth cries out for vengeance; that evil violates a natural harmony which only retribution can restore; that a wronged collectivity owes a duty to the moral order to punish the criminal' (Yosal Rogat). And yet I think it is undeniable that it was precisely on the ground of these long forgotten propositions that Eichmann was brought to justice to begin with, and that they were, in fact, the supreme justification for the death penalty.[13]

Justice is possible because there are certain limits to human action that we expect all human beings to recognize, no matter what situation they are in. If they fail to act justly and commit crimes against others, then they have failed to meet the universal conditions of our living together in the world. If a whole state such as Nazi Germany or Stalinist Russia becomes criminal in its activity, this does not mean that justice has fled the world. It means that those states have failed to recognize the universal standards of behaviour. Since the universal standards remain constant, we can reasonably expect that any individual who thinks and reflects on his being human can still behave justly within such a state. Eichmann was justly condemned, in Arendt's view, because he failed to behave in an *essentially* human way. In the following passage Arendt suggests that Eichmann should have been capable of judgment independent of, and regardless of, the political situation in which he found himself: 'What we have demanded in these trials [of war criminals] is that human beings be capable of telling right from wrong even when all they have to guide them is their own judgment which, moreover, happens to be completely at odds with what they must regard as the unanimous opinion of all those around them.'[14] This view put her in a position of having to defend a transcendent conception of justice for which her previous work had made no provision.

Arendt condemned Eichmann for his acts, but what bothered her was his 'thoughtlessness.' This lack of thought appeared to her to have something to do with his inability to recognize that he had committed criminal acts.[15] Arendt thereby inferred that the capacity for thought was prerequisite for the exercise of political judgment, and perhaps for recognizing justice. Not community, not 'public space,' but the interior, private activity of reflective thought is necesary for freedom. Finally, Arendt was compelled to admit that the capacity for meaningful thought is not dependent upon shared meaning for its existence. If it were, we would have no effective way of resisting totalitarianism, and we certainly could not judge anyone whose words and deeds were shaped by it. The denial of public discourse, the prevalence of ideology, and the widespread use of terror, despite their cumulative effect, do not excuse Eichmann's actions. He can be judged because we adhere to certain 'truths' or 'essences' that stand outside politics and are discoverable through thought alone.

Arendt wrote the essay 'Truth and Politics' as an explicit response to her own book on Eichmann. The essay was meant to reintroduce considerations of truth into her understanding of politics, considerations that had been excluded deliberately in *The Human Condition*. It treads carefully over this new territory, and for good reason. Arendt had always been wary of the bond between 'truth-tellers' – philosophers, historians, and poets – and the political realm, for the reasons discussed in chapter 1. Truth is coercive; politics is persuasive. Truth relies upon 'givens'; politics is the realm of 'creating anew.' Previously, Arendt could not see any way to introduce the compelling force of truth into the political realm without destroying freedom. Now, however, she was confronted with a dilemma. If one did not introduce 'truths' into politics, either philosophic or factual, how could one judge the activities of a community that had become totalitarian? How could one expect an individual to act contrary to the opinions of that community?

The essay on truth and politics is somewhat ambiguous about the precise relationship between its two subjects. It focuses on two kinds of truth, one perceived by the theorist through reason and the other recorded by the story-teller or the historian. What they have in common is their standpoint 'outside the political realm.'[16] They are pursued in solitude, from the vantage point of the spectator who has withdrawn from the world of action. Significantly, the one characteristic that is absolutely necessary in the pursuit of truth is the capacity to think.

However tentative this essay might have been, it seems that a dramatic reversal had taken place in Arendt's thought. Contrary to her earlier claims that the sphere of political action was autonomous, she here wrote that the political realm, 'its greatness notwithstanding,' is 'limited by those things which men cannot change at will.'[17] The things that men cannot change include not only the natural limitations of human life, but also the capacity to reflect upon them and translate that reflection into an understanding of good and bad actions.

Thought, Truth, and Moral Considerations

It cannot be overemphasized just how much of a radical break Arendt made from her early 'political' works in turning her attention to questions of truth and morality. She had excluded any considerations of the interior life from her early works on the grounds that this 'life' is less real than the appearances of speech and deed. In *The Human Condition*, for example, she wrote: 'Compared with the reality which comes from being seen and heard, even the greatest forces of intimate life – the passions of the heart, the thoughts of the mind, the delights of the senses – lead an uncertain, shadowy kind of existence unless and until they are transformed, deprivatized and deindividualized, as it were, into a shape to fit them for public appearance.'[18] Arendt characterized both love and philosophic thought as 'unworldy, invisible' activities. Religious as well as philosophic love have a 'non-human, supernatural quality.'[19] The love of God or truth, which has been the outstanding motivation behind much of the Western philosophic tradition, she regarded as a negation of, or solipsistic retreat from, the world of appearances: 'Fleeing the world and hiding from its inhabitants, it negates the space the world offers to men and most of all that public part of it where everything and everybody are seen and heard by all.'[20]

Arendt thought that the retreat into interiority was a wilful abdication of one's responsibilities to the world and to other men; and she did not discriminate among different kinds of 'interiority.' In the face of totalitarianism, for example, she did not see much difference between the solipsistic wanderings of the philosophers and the political indifference of the average bourgeois citizen. In either case the consequence was what Arendt called an 'inner emigration' as an inappropriate response to the events of Nazi domination. 'How tempting it was,' Arendt wrote, 'simply to ignore the intolerably stupid blabber of the Nazis. But seductive though it may be to yield to such temptations and to hole up in the refuge of one's own psyche, the result will always be a loss of humanness along with the forsaking of reality.'[22]

Arendt did not sustain her disdain of the interior realm after she thought about Eichmann. Instead, she realized that one had to distinguish between the 'inner emigration' prompted by the need to think and that of the bourgeois. It is not sufficient to look simply at the effect – a turning away from the political realm – one must also examine the motives for doing so. Arendt's change of attitude towards 'inner emigration' is perhaps best illustrated in her apparent reassessment of Martin Heidegger in the last years of her life. In her early account of Heidegger's response to events in Germany in the 1930s, as we know, Arendt was angry and judgmental towards Heidegger for his support of National Socialism. 'He entered the Nazi Party in a very sensational way in 1933,' a move that Arendt attributed to Heidegger's 'desperation' and 'delusion of genius.'[23] Later, of course, Heidegger withdrew his support from the party, abdicated his chair at Freiburg University (to which he had been appointed by the Nazis as a replacement for Husserl), and retreated from politics altogether. A younger Arendt would probably have condemned Heidegger as much for this retreat into private life as she had for his initial foray into politics. As Elisabeth Young-Bruehl notes, Arendt had allied herself with Karl Jaspers – a thinker to whom community, friendship, dialogue, and plurality were the formative contexts of philosophizing – against 'the tradition of solitary philosophizing far from the world and from others,' a tradition that Heidegger exemplified.[24] This alliance with Jaspers, against Heidegger, is clear in Arendt's early study of 'Existenz philosophy.'

Yet, late in her life, Arendt wrote an essay on the occasion of Heidegger's eightieth birthday, praising his contributions to philosophy and offering what amounted to an apology for Heidegger's political 'error' in collaborating with the Nazis. She compared Heidegger's brief enthusiasm for National Socialism with Plato's attempt to counsel the tyrant of Syracuse. She wrote that we 'can hardly help finding it striking and perhaps exasperating that Plato and Heidegger, when they entered into human affairs, turned to tyrants and Führers,'[25] and suggested that bad political judgment is a *déformation professionelle* that we have come to expect from solitary thinkers. What is also strikingly similar about Plato and Heidegger, according to Arendt, is that they quickly learned the error of their ways and retreated permanently to the inner sanctum of the thinking abode, which was their 'natural' home. With respect to Heidegger, Arendt said: 'He was still young enough to learn from the shock of the collision, which after ten short, hectic months thirty-seven years ago drove him back to his residence, and to settle in his thinking what he had experienced.'[26] Arendt looked upon this retreat as an entirely appropriate response, since thinking, as she says explicitly in this essay on Heidegger, requires an 'essential seclusion from the world.'[27]

The implications of the essay on Heidegger seem obvious. Arendt suggests that it was Heidegger's venture into the limelight of the public realm that distorted his capacity for judgment, and that his good sense was restored only when he retreated from the public realm back into his own solitary thoughts. Unlike Eichmann, who did not think at all and who never considered that he had made any errors in judgment, Heidegger's error and his recognition of it led him to seek solitude where he could reflect upon his experience. Arendt's final judgment on Heidegger written in 1971, in contrast to her earlier critique of him in 1946, praises his contribution to philosophy. Ultimately, she said, for Heidegger, as for those few great thinkers who have discovered in solitude the intrinsic worth of thinking, 'it does not matter where the storms of [his] century may have driven [him].'[28] What Heidegger made manifestly clear was that the inner emigration of the philosopher is not an escape from responsibility to the world, but rather is a prerequisite for thinking: 'compared with other places in the world, the habitations of human affairs, the residence of the thinker is a "place of stillness." '[29]

Once Arendt had put forward the notion that thinking, rather than the public space, might be the prerequisite for good judgment in politics, she felt compelled to reassess the nature of the interior life and the withdrawal that characterizes all thinking. Thinking demands withdrawal from the world, as has been said since the beginnings of the Western philosophic tradition. It was Aristotle who wrote that 'the wise man can contemplate by himself, and the more so the wiser he is.'[30] As another writer put it, Plato suggested that truth and meaning are 'to be found only in the lived real moment of direct apprehension out of which the indirectness of mimetic art and writing and perhaps language and discursive thought itself always tends to remove us.'[31]

In her essay on truth and politics Arendt was concerned to 'prove' the existence of things that do not appear in the world and cannot be demonstrated even in speech. She talked specifically about the Socratic proposition that is is better to suffer wrong than to do wrong, a proposition that Socrates was incapable of demonstrating in the market-place, where all claims are treated as opinions. Yet, as Arendt said: 'To the philosopher – or, rather, to man insofar as he is a thinking being – this ethical proposition about doing and suffering wrong is no less compelling than mathematical truth.'[32] The Socratic proposition, even given its undemonstrable and intensely private nature, may have a direct bearing on the behaviour of the individual in political life: 'though one may doubt that it ever had a direct political consequence, its impact upon practical conduct as an ethical precept is undeniable.'[33] The impact of thought on the political realm has been felt, said Arendt, not through any application of doctrine or principle, for this will always fail, but rather in the example of thinking human beings whose conduct is exemplary. Even though she maintained that the link between thought and action was an indirect one, she nevertheless acknowledged that the 'hiddenness' of thought may be a crucial factor in knowing how to act: that thought may be more important than 'public space' as the foundation of good judgment about the world.

The Life of the Mind is about this 'region' of thought, about the hidden, un-appearing processes that take place in any human being. It is not a political work, as Arendt would have defined political, because it is concerned with the solitariness of thinking; but Arendt felt that it was necessary, finally, to explore the nature of thought in order to understand how people act politically. Always impatient with the rational constructions of philosophy, she seemed prepared in her final work to reassess the question of 'being' and metaphysics. In many respects, *The Life of the Mind* may have been a disappointment to Arendt's readers. Accustomed to her often brilliant, always brash statements about politics and action, the reader might find this project subdued and rambling. Arendt was much more tentative about her final project, probably because much of what she wrote contradicted her own earlier statements. *The Life of the Mind* is unquestionably an implicit refutation of much of what she said in *The Human Condition*. In the latter work she had tried to dissociate action from other human activities – labour, work, and thought – but in the former she concluded that this separation of activities could not be maintained. At the end of the second volume, entitled *Willing*, Arendt resigned herself to the fact that her prior isolation of action from thought had been misguided: 'When we directed our attention to men of action, hoping to find in them a notion of freedom purged of the perplexities caused for men's minds by the reflexivity of mental activities ... we hoped for more than we finally achieved.'[34] In looking solely at action, in the hopes of there discovering a kind of freedom that is unburdened by the restrictions of thought, Arendt had been searching for an account from those 'who ought to be committed to freedom because of the very nature of their activity, which consists in "changing the world," and not in interpreting or knowing it.'[35] She found instead that the legends of political foundation, attempting to account for freedom of action, faced an 'abyss of nothingness that opens up before any deed that cannot be accounted for by a reliable chain of cause and effect.'[36]

In attempting to rethink the place of thought in action and politics, Arendt was drawn to questions of teleology. In spite of her lifelong commitment to freedom, Arendt declared in *The Life of the Mind* that men cannot act ex nihilo. To claim an 'absolute beginning' (or an 'absolute end') is nonsensical, not because we cannot act in this fashion, but because it would be tantamount to 'thinking the unthinkable.'[37] If action is not curtailed by thought in some way, it may have disastrous consequences for the world. Arendt realized that one could go too far in praising the freedom and unbridled spontaneity of human action. The ramifications of 'freedom abused' are felt in the modern world not only in the unhappy outcomes of revolutions, but also in the advances in technology made by men who believe that they can fashion the world in any manner they wish. Modern science and technology, according to Arendt, have come precariously close to creating new forms of life. Technology has enabled men to 'handle nature from a point in the universe outside the earth.'[38] By 'releas[ing] energy processes that ordinarily go on only in the sun,' by 'attempt[ing] to initiate in a test-tube the processes of cosmic evolution,' and by performing other such 'unnatural' feats, modern man is transgressing some sort of natural law. Arendt said that the scientists of our age may be 'perilously close' to making it possible to destroy the stature of man.[39] From this point of view, what technology and totalitarianism have in common is their ability to do unprecedented things. Technology can initiate radically new processes, that is, it can make new beginnings; and totalitarianism perpetrates genocide, that is, it brings about absolute ends. Moreover, Arendt linked totalitarians and technocrats together by saying that neither think. When Arendt asked why Eichmann perpetrated crimes against humanity, the only answer she could provide was that he did not think. Similarly, in reflecting upon the dangers of technological innovation, Arendt wrote that 'the very integrity of science demands that not only utilitarian considerations but the reflection upon the stature of man as well be left in abeyance.'[40] The trouble with 'scientifically-minded brain trusters' is 'not that they are cold-blooded enough to "think the unthinkable," but that they do not *think*.'[41]

What Arendt was seeking, then, was an understanding of thinking that can prohibit what can only be called immoral action. Clearly, she thought that some forms of action transgress a 'sacred' limitation although she could not give an account of the limitation or how it is to be apprehended. She needed an understanding of thinking that distinguished it from action – that is, one in which thinking could be judgmental of action –but that also somehow allowed for freedom. She sought a definition of thought that did not accept the coercive demands of truth, but that could still serve as a guide to human action. Though Arendt identified various forms of evil with non-thinking, she wondered what kind of thinking is necessary for making good judgments. Thinking in itself does not necessarily lead to good judgment, as Arendt made manifestly clear in her article on Existenz philosophy. Understanding the limitations of action and the difference between right and wrong requires something more.

In her article 'Thinking and Moral Considerations' – which Arendt's friend Glenn Gray described as the 'precursor of the [then] unpublished *Life of the Mind*'[42] – Arendt established three clear guidelines for 'the inner connection between the ability or inability to think and the problem of evil':[43]

> *First*, if such a connection exists at all, then the knowledge of thinking, as distinguished from the thirst for knowledge, must be ascribed to everybody; it cannot be a privilege of the few.
>
> *Second*, if Kant is right and the faculty of thought has a 'natural aversion' against accepting its own results as 'solid axioms,' then we cannot expect any moral propositions or commandments, no final code of conduct from the thinking activity, least of all a new and now allegedly final decision of what is good and what is evil.
>
> *Third*, if it is true that thinking deals with invisibles, it follows that it is out of order because we normally move in a world of appearances in which the most radical experience of disappearance is death. The gift for dealing with things that do not appear has often been believed to exact a price – the price of binding the thinker or the poet to the visible world. Think of Homer, whom the gods gave the divine gift by striking him with blindness; think of Plato's *Phaedo* where those who do philosophy appear to those who don't, the many, like people who pursue death. Think of Zeno, the founder of Stoicism, who asked the Delphic Oracle what he should do to attain the best life and was answered, 'Take on the color of the dead.'[44]

In short, Arendt established that whatever connection thinking has with the prevention of evil action, it has to be universal in all human beings, non-prescriptive, and non-dogmatic; and that it is a hidden capacity that does not appear in particular acts or words. Particularly striking in the third of Arendt's propositions, is the likening of the experience of thinking to death. We know that Arendt had been disturbed throughout much of her life by the metaphorical description of thinking as a kind of 'dying,' yet we see here how much she was moved by the consistency and power of such images. Though essential for living, and for making judgments about the living, thinking seems to entail an eclipse of the world.[45]

There is not much in these three considerations on the nature of thought that discloses the connection between thinking and 'doing the good,' but Arendt would say that this is as much as can be said about a quality that resides in the realm of 'non-appearance.' She could only refer to an example to clarify her thoughts on the matter. She cited Socrates, a man 'who did think without becoming a philosopher, a citizen among citizens, doing nothing, claiming nothing that, in his view, every citizen should do and had a right to claim.'[46] Socrates was quite content to go about the market-place talking about things such as justice, for which he had no answer. Arendt asked herself how the 'winds of thought' – which are neither demonstrative in their 'proof' nor persuasive in the realm of opinion – could possibly produce any beneficial effect for the person who thinks or on those who encounter a man like Socrates.

The essay on thinking and moral considerations does not answer this question; it expresses Arendt's considerations on the whole matter of thought. Arendt knew full well that 'thinking,' as she described it, could have the obverse effect of enciting people to cynicism and confusion, for thinking questions the authority of all opinions without providing a corrective for wrong ones. Socrates avoided the 'dangerous' consequences of thinking by associating it with a kind of love: since one can love only the good and the beautiful, thought is by definition the dwelling on the good and the beautiful. For Socrates, evil has no essence of its own. Men who 'do evil' are simply ignorant or wayward souls who do not know what the good is. In this sense, evil is a negation, or better, a mere absence of the good. It is unintelligible because it has no object. Arendt rejected the association of evil with 'absence' because she thought that it implied that only those with Plato's 'noble nature' are equipped to think.[47]

In contrast to what she thought was the exclusivity of the noble nature that loves the good, Arendt drew from the example of Socrates a second, more tentative explanaton of the 'thinking ego.' This second account she called the 'two-in-one,' by which she meant the inner dialogue between me and myself, or the 'difference given in consciousness.'[48] Arendt characterized the 'two-in-one' as a partnership between consciousness and thought. She claimed that the experience of inner duality was just that: an experience common to everyone who wrestles with ideas, and not some axiomatic theory about how moral propositions are formulated. The notion that every man has a conscience that is in conflict with his deeds, for example, stems from this experience.

The 'two-in-one' of thinking, this 'conscience' that battles with deeds, is what Arendt thought held the key to understanding the connection between the inner life of the mind and the performance of good or evil deeds in the world. The two-in-one never appears in the public realm – 'for others, ... I appear as one and the same'[49] – but its actualization in the hidden regions of the mind can have serious political consequences. The political and moral significance of the inner dialogue of thought manifests itself in times of political crisis when those who think are conspicuous in their refusal to participate. At such times, she said, thinking does become a kind of political action because it is the precursor of judgment. Arendt's final word in the essay on thinking and moral considerations is also a prefatory schema to *The Life of the Mind*:

> If thinking, the two-in-one of the soundless dialogue, actualizes the difference
> within our identity as given in consciousness and thereby results in conscience
> as its by-product, then judging, the by-product of the liberating effect of thinking,
> realizes thinking, makes it manifest in the world of appearances, where I am
> never alone and always much too busy to be able to think. The manifestation of the
> wind of thought is no knowledge: it is the ability to tell right from wrong,
> beautiful from ugly. And this indeed may prevent catastrophes, at least for myself,
> in the rare moments when the chips are down.[50]

The two-in-one thinking is an intriguing way of describing the thinking process, but it is difficult to see how Arendt's formulation of it has anything to do with 'moral considerations.' She insisted that thought is not prescriptive, that in itself it does not make moral judgments, and that within itself it harbours the danger of nihilism since it is capable of dissolving all conventions and values: 'Thinking is equally dangerous to all creeds and, by itself, does not bring forth any new creed.'[51] She wanted to preserve the Socratic notion of the two-in-one, but at the same time to divorce 'conscience' from the Socratic grounding in the love of the good. The result is a rather empty conception of the nature of thought.

Surely, by referring to the identity and difference of consciousness Arendt did not mean to suggest a kind of rational, calculating dialogue. She was searching for a definition of thought that could provide meaning and some sort of moral sensibility, if not specific prescriptions for action. It is also curious that she rejected the Socratic association of thought with eros on the sole ground that it would necessarily restrict thinking to those few who have a 'noble' nature. Though she wrote at the end of *The Human Condition* that, as a 'living experience, thought has always been assumed, perhaps wrongly, to be known only to the few,'[52] she was quite aware that the experience of philosophic thought has been rare among men in all times. She wanted to believe that the rarity of thought was a contingent factor: something occasioned by the cloistered protectionism of 'professional thinkers' and the circumstances associated with the decline of the public realm. She also wanted to believe that the experience of thought could be opened to all men, if these barriers to it could be broken down. Her task in *The Life of the Mind* was to determine 'what makes us think,' and by demystifying philosophy she hoped to lay the foundations for the re-awakening of the experience of thought. Arendt wrote in the introduction to *The Life of the Mind*: 'If ... the ability to tell right from wrong should turn out to have anything to do with the ability to think, then we must be able to "demand" its exercise from every sane person, no matter how erudite or ignorant, intelligent or stupid, he may happen to be.'[53] Arendt hoped that she would be able to make the connection between thinking and acting, and that her findings would make it evident that we can demand thought from every sane person. Ultimately, this was her last attempt to counteract totalitarianism.

4 *The Life of the Mind*

The Schematic

The explorations that Arendt made in her essay 'Thinking and Moral Considerations' were expanded into what was to be her most difficult work: *The Life of the Mind*. The three imperatives of thought she sketched in that essay remain the central commitment of this last work, but they carried Arendt into a type of analysis that is not foreshadowed in the essay: a breakdown of the structure of the mind into three separate faculties.

The Life of the Mind was intended to be a three-part study, each section devoted to the examination of one faculty. What we have is a volume called 'Thinking' and one on 'Willing.' A projected third, on 'Judging,' was not completed before Arendt's death, although there is enough substance on the subject from scattered remarks made in the first two volumes, and from a set of lecture notes prepared as a groundwork for 'Judging,' for us to extrapolate what this final volume might have looked like. The first question one is prompted to ask, when confronted with this tripartite structure, is: Why did Arendt conceive of the life of the mind as a fragmented process? It has been noted by almost all her critics that she had an inclination to divide activities of any sort into separate (and often tripartite) categories. In *The Human Condition*, for example, she divided all 'worldly' activities into labour, work, and action. But there one can see some correlation between theoretical classification and phenomena. The same cannot be said for the activities of the mind. No matter what happens in consciousness, as Arendt said, we always appear in the world as one unitary being.[1] The differences given in consciousness do not *appear*; if they do exist, they have to be evident within the structure of the mind itself.

What is the life of the mind, then, if not something that discloses itself in worldly activity? Arendt wrote in the introduction to 'Thinking' that human beings have always been thinking beings and by this she meant simply the following: 'Men have an inclination, perhaps a need, to think beyond the limitations of knowledge, to do more with this ability than use it as an instrument for knowing and doing.'[2] In other words, thinking performs some task other than its utilitarian service to the world in the pursuit of practical ends. In fact, according to Arendt, when thinking goes beyond the limitations of knowledge, it *contradicts* the reality of the world of appearances: 'Thinking ... which subjects everything it gets hold of to doubt, has no such natural, matter-of-fact relation to reality.'[3] Reality, in this context, meant for Arendt the world as given to us through sense perception. This 'reality' has a truth content that we trust implicitly and we assume that others share the same trust. Arendt had another term for the whole sphere governed by the trust in perception. She called it the world of common sense and she was quite sure that there existed within the mind a sort of intramural warfare between the comlacency of common sense and the inquisitive doubt of 'thinking,' which subjects everything that crosses its path to examination.

I think it was this intramural warfare of the mind that led Arendt to conceptualize the working of the mind as being divided into distinct faculties. She wanted to know how it is possible for a human being to discern when it is appropriate to let common sense govern us, and when it is necessary to forgo common sense for the much more opaque business of 'thinking.' What is required is an explanation of how the mind shifts from one *kind* of thinking to another. Even if Arendt called the capacity to move among the world of appearances 'common sense,' she certainly did not mean by this some kind of instinct or sensual response. Common sense is a particular sort of thinking: the sort that is necessary for practical living. 'Thinking,' in contradistinction to common sense, is the quest for meaning. The problem is: when the stability of the world of common sense is threatened (as happened under the duress of totalitarian rule), where is the locale for an alternative type of thinking? Arendt put the matter succinctly. If I am in possession of a concept that criticizes some aspect of appearance, from where do I get this concept if not from the world of appearances itself? In thinking specifically about the concept 'the banality of evil,' Arendt remarked, 'I could not help raising the *quaestio juris* and asking myself "by what right I possessed and used it?" '[4]

The problem is perhaps made clearer by Paul Ricoeur in his reflections on *The Human Condition*.[5] Ricoeur maintains that the major difficulty in this early work was Arendt's refusal to come to terms with thought. To Ricoeur, it is obvious that Arendt could not have made the distinctions betwen the *vita activa* and the *vita contemplativa* unless she had some notion of the 'enduring teleological condition' that governs the human condition: 'It is *vita contemplativa* which allows *vita activa* to understand itself and to reflect upon its own temporal condition.'[6] To think about the human condition in all its aspects of appearance – in labour, work, and action – requires that we are able to view these appearances from a standpoint that is not subjected to the flux of history. As Ricoeur put it: 'Eternity is what is lacking to mortals but to the extent that we think we think eternity. (We might even say that to think *is* to think eternity.)'[7]

Arendt, I am certain, would have objected to Ricoeur's equation of thinking and eternity because the association conjures up too many unsuitable images from the history of philosophy, wherein thinking has been attached to the experience of the divine or a realm of human 'essences' that stands outside the appearing world. Nevertheless, Ricoeur has singled out the fundamental issue: How does Arendt account for the ability of thought to discriminate among appearances if she believes that the sole referent of the human being is his constitution as an appearance?

Arendt, of course, was fully aware of her dilemma by the time she wrote *The Life of the Mind*.[8] She did not want to give up her belief that appearance is the primary 'condition' of being human, but she had to account for the capacity to think, which is, somehow, outside this condition. She attempted to facilitate her task by assigning separate faculties to different dimensions of experience. Volume 1, on 'Thinking,' addresses the activity of the mind that flees the world of appearance. In trying to capture the essence of this faculty, Arendt cited P.F. Strawson on Kant, in a passage that echoes Ricoeur's thoughts. 'It is indeed an old belief,' said Strawson, that 'reason is something essentially outside of time and yet in us.'[9] Bothered by this old belief, Arendt proposed to determine whether such claims 'are caused by dogmatic beliefs and arbitrary assumptions, mere mirages that disappear upon closer inspection, or whether they are inherent in the paradoxical condition of a living being that, though itself part of the world of appearances, is in possession of a faculty, the ability to think, that permits the mind to withdraw from the world without ever being able to leave or transcend it.'[10]

The work on 'Thinking' is the one farthest removed in spirit from any of Arendt's earlier works for it concentrates entirely upon the hidden process of thought. The remaining two volumes of *The Life of the Mind* are closer to Arendt's other writings because she attached 'Willing' and 'Judging' to man's being a creature of the world. In her own words, willing and judging 'deal with particulars and in this respect are much closer to the realm of appearances.'[11] More precisely, willing and judging each correspond to a predominant experience that man has as a being in time. Willing turns on the future, on matters that 'are not yet,' and judging is the faculty for dealing with the past, matters that 'are no more.'[12] The situation of all human beings between past and future was, for Arendt, the stance of the actor who must always gauge the practical possibilities for the future and, in so doing, must simultaneously take stock of the past. Willing and judging had for her a kind of solidity – a matter-of-fact quality – that thinking lacks. They are the kindred faculties of common sense. The overall project of *The Life of the Mind* was to provide a synthetic view of the mind's ability to hold what Ricoeur called the 'eternity' of thought and the temporality of willing and judging in a compatible union.

We will begin, as Arendt did, with thinking: what she termed the 'small, inconspicuous track of non-time ... within the time-space given to natal and mortal men.'[13] Though Arendt insisted that each of the faculties of the mind is autonomous, she conceded that there is an order of priorities among them. Thinking for her was primary, as she stated unequivocally in the following passage: 'It is inconceivable how we would ever be able to will or to judge, that is, to handle things which are not yet and things which are no more, if the power of representation and the effort necessary to direct mental activities to what in every way escapes the attention of sense perception had not gone ahead and prepared the mind for further reflection as well as for willing and judging.'[14]

Thinking

Thinking posed a special problem for Arendt, as we know, because of her overriding attachment to the world of appearances and her predisposition towards the sense of reality provided by common sense. Whereas all other activities, including the mind's activities of willing and judging, rely upon the existence of a shared world, thinking's need is quite the opposite: 'For thinking ... withdrawal from the world of appearances is the *only* essential precondition.'[15] The stillness and withdrawal that characterizes thinking struck Arendt as being so much out of the ordinary realm of human experience that she empathized with those who depict it as an activity 'contrary to the human condition.'[16]

Arendt assumed that the strangeness of thought is experienced by all those who have ever 'stopped to think,' but it is the professional thinker who is most troubled by it. It is the sensation of being removed from the world that has led philosophers to construct the two-worlds theories of body and mind, being and becoming, essence and appearance. It is as though when faced with the opposite experiences of self – one 'being in the world' and another escaping into thought – the philosopher feels compelled to rank them. Second-order realities give a home to the thinking ego. It did not seem odd to Arendt that so many professional thinkers had compared the experience of thought to dying. From Plato – 'philosophy is the practice of dying' – to Schopenhauer – 'death actually is the inspiring genius of philosophy' – the analogy has persisted, perhaps because death, like thought, is contrary to the business of the living.

Though the comparison of thinking to death was comprehensible to Arendt, she rejected the analogy, saying that it dwelled too intensely on only one aspect of experience to the neglect of the other, more 'worldly' activities of the mind. The philosopher who quits the city of men for the 'truer' reality of thought is forcing himself to abandon his natural habitat among other people. Arendt could not accept that the realm of thought provided a more meaningful experience than that provided by the senses, for as she reminded her readers often, human beings are born into the world as beings who appear for others, and this appearance is the first condition of all life, including the life of the philosopher.[17] She frequently cited Descartes's great error in asserting his dictum: 'I think, therefore I am.' The 'I am' is implied in the 'I think,' as Arendt said, and is the condition of Descartes's being able to think at all. That Descartes could make such a mistake confirmed for Arendt just how onerous an undertaking it has been for philosophers to deal with the dualism of world and thought. Descartes's folly was 'to hope he could overcome his doubt by insisting on withdrawing from the world altogether, eliminating every worldly reality and concentrating only on the thinking activity itself.'[18]

Not only Descartes's proposed resolution, but any 'solution' to the problem of thinking that posited a transcendent object, was rejected by Arendt. Though thinking is always out of order, compared with the ordinary course of events, it is not so unworldly that its object is extra-human. According to Arendt, thinking has no object other than its own activity. 'Looked at from the perspective of the everyday world of appearances, the everywhere of the thinking ego – summoning into its presence whatever it pleases from any distance in time and space, which thought traverses with a velocity greater than light's – is a *nowhere*.'[19]

As proof that thought is inherently bound to the world of appearances, and not to some other-worldly object, Arendt appealed to the structure of language. Whatever content thought has, she wrote, it can be revealed only in speech for 'thinking beings have an urge to speak and speaking beings have an urge to think.'[20] The withdrawal of thought is always recalled to the world in the need of human beings to make themselves understood, and philosophers have always tried to communicate their thoughts through the use of metaphor, that is, by referring to the things of the world. One of the richest metaphors bequeathed to us by the tradition of thought is Plato's description of philosophy as a blinding vision: since Plato, Arendt wrote, all philosophic terms have been 'frozen analogies.'[21] In Arendt's understanding of things, the frozen analogy achieves 'carrying-over' from the realm of thought to the realm of being an 'appearance among appearances.'[22] The link of metaphorical language meant for Arendt that thought has no 'home' other than the world. 'Analogies, metaphors and emblems are the threads by which the mind holds on to the world even when, absentmindedly, it has lost direct contact with it, and they guarantee the unity of human experience.'[23]

The arguments that Arendt makes for the link between thought and world (forged by metaphor) are convincing, but they do not account for the unqiue experience of thinking: they show only how thought is brought back to the world, not why it leaves the world in the first place. Arendt did try to explain in *The Life of the Mind* why thought retreats from the sensual world, and she gives two different accounts. The first is an elaboration of her discussion of the 'two-in-one' of consciousness, first set out in 'Thinking and Moral Considerations.' It is an attempt to describe the need to think as an enduring 'gift' of consciousness. The second account locates the urge to think in a temporal sequence, and in this account Arendt describes thought as the meeting point between past and future. I will try to outline what is involved in each of these accounts and to explain what the connection is between them.

We have to keep in mind that Arendt wanted to avoid a transcendent account of thought's object. She acknowledged the importance of reflective thought for making judgments about the world, but she was not willing to sacrifice the integrity of the world for the sake of a clear picture of thought. In trying to locate thought in something that is enduring, yet immanent, Arendt turned to the elusive Socratic formulation of thinking as a dialogue 'between me and myself.' Thinking may be a withdrawal from the plurality of the world, but for Arendt the retreat into solitude meant that we have the opportunity to converse with ourselves. The introspection of thought is sparked by a discomfiting sense that one's conscience is not at peace. The job of thinking is to bring the two discordant halves of conscience back into harmony with one another so that when one emerges from this inner dialogue back into the world, one can be truly at one with oneself. In the account of thinking as the 'two-in-one,' Arendt must have been conceiving of thinking as a moral activity. What draws a person into thought initially is the apprehension that a wrong has been committed. As an example of what she meant by the inner dialogue of thought, Arendt quoted at length a soliloquy from Shakespeare's Richard III, in which Richard is at war with himself. Having committed murder, he is afraid not of punishment but of the revenge of his own psyche.[24] Though Arendt claimed that thinking *in itself* is not prompted by moral considerations, she said that the man who does not struggle for internal harmony is incapable of making moral judgments. The interconnections between thinking and moral judgment are evident in the following passage: 'A person who does not know ... silent intercourse (in which we examine what we say and what we do) will not mind contradicting himself, and this means he will never be either able or willing to account for what he says or does; nor will he mind committing any crime since he can count on its being forgotten the next moment. Bad people are *not* "full of regrets." '[25]

This is where Arendt ended her discussion of the 'two-in-one' of thinking. There is no conclusion as to what the force is within us that plagues us with doubt and conscience, nor is there any explanation of why some people feel the need to resolve the inner contradictions of thought and some perceive no conflict at all. We know that Arendt resisted the Socratic axiom that people who think are those who love 'the good.' She also resisted anything like a psychoanalytic explanation of thinking as the struggle between 'id' and 'ego.' The trouble with modern psychology, she wrote, is that even though it differs from metaphysical explanations of the object of the thinking ego in that it locates the object in the individual psyche rather than in some transcendent realm, it none the less reduces the source of thinking to a single, determinate 'essence': the supposedly uncontrollable passions. By making the 'sameness' of passions and instincts the ground of 'truth,' psychology minimizes the importance of the freedom of thinking. Psychology thus commits the same error as metaphysical thinking, according to Arendt, in that it diminishes the significance of the *thinking person* and exalts some hidden force as the basis of thought. She dismissed modern psychology's account of the split within the psyche in the following manner: 'The monotonous sameness and pervasive ugliness so highly characteristic of the findings of modern psychology, and contrasting so obviously with the enormous variety and richness of overt human conduct, witness to the radical difference between the inside and outside of the human body ... Without the sexual urge, arising out of our reproductive organs, love would not be possible; but while the urge is always the same, how great is the variety in the actual appearances of love!'[26]

We have established that whatever the 'ground' of thinking may have been for Arendt, it was nothing fixed and absolute, neither a transcendent order of 'being' nor some hidden, determinate force within the psyche. The inner dialogue of thought could not be explained for her by locating some natural and eternal 'essence' against which human beings struggle. Yet she did speak of essences. 'A life without thinking,' she wrote, 'is quite possible,' but such a life '*fails to develop its own essence* – it is not merely meaningless, it is not fully alive.'[27]

The appeal to 'essence' seems to contradict everything that Arendt had written about thinking. But in fact, in talking about the 'essence' of being human, Arendt pointed back to her preoccupation with man's temporality. The last segment of 'Thinking' begins with a cryptic parable of Kafka's through which Arendt tries to explain the place of thinking in the time spectrum given to man. This is her second attempt to account for thinking, and here she referred to thought as the activity contained by the boundary concepts of past and future.

From the standpoint of 'being-in-the-world,' Arendt said that our understanding of our place is that of being inserted 'between an infinite past and an infinite future.' Transposed between the 'no more' and the 'not yet,' we have the dualistic sensations of being determined by all that has come before us, yet having the confidence that the future is ours to shape as we will. In the sensation of being alive, man is forced to reckon with these two fundamentally antagonistic forces: 'Man lives in this in-between, and what he calls the present is a life-long fight against the dead weight of the past, driving him forward with hope, and the fear of a future (whose only certainty is death), driving him backward toward the "quiet of the past" with nostalgia and remembrance of the only reality he can be sure of.'[28]

Seen only from the vantage point of the place human beings occupy in a linear time sequence, the clash of past and future seems to be an irreconcilable one. Its outcome would be tragic, for no matter what plans we may shape for the future, we know that these future deeds will always become a part of the past and will serve as the limitations upon the conduct of future generations. The sense of being locked between past and future is the defining characteristic of the human condition for Arendt, but it is not necessarily a tragic position. Thinking is the means whereby human beings can avoid tragedy. Thinking is the monumental effort on the part of individuals to resist seeing themselves as either the pawns of history or the all-powerful creators of the future. The thinking being actualizes his 'essence' by weighing the counterposed forces of past and future, incorporating both in his mind but never succumbing to one or the other. This is surely what Arendt must have meant in the following passage where she summed up her thoughts on thinking:

> Each new generation, every new human being, as he becomes conscious of being inserted between an infinite past and an infinite future, must discover and ploddingly pave anew the path of thought. And it is after all possible, and seems to be likely, that the strange survival of great works, their relative permanence throughout thousands of years, is due to their having been born in the small, inconspicuous track of non-time which their authors' thought had beaten between an infinite past and an infinite future by accepting past and future as directed, aimed, as it were, at themselves ... thus establishing a present for themselves, a kind of timeless time in which men are able to create timeless works with which to transcend their own finiteness.[29]

The moral content of thinking, as I understand it, is the moderation of one who is able to contain within his mind all the given boundaries of his existence. He is not overcome with excessive apprehension or greed for the future; and he is not grieved with melancholy for the determinations of the past over which he has no control. In other words, he does not resent his being a creature of time. The inner dialogue of thinking, then, is an ability to summon the given condition of one's existence into consciousness. This is why, for Arendt, 'Willing' – the faculty oriented towards the future – and 'Judging' – the faculty for evaluating the past –

were instrumental in the constitution of the life of the mind. While each of them, in its singularity, emphasizes only one dimension of experience, taken together they form the context in which thinking is formulated. Without them, thinking runs amok into a fantasy world. The 'two-in-one' of thinking, in which I experience some sort of internal diremption, happens when one of the circumscribing conditions of my life – either willing or judging – has taken over and dominated the psyche. In this case, it is necessary to withdraw from the turmoil of the world long enough to set the psyche in order, to balance the faculties.

Willing

The faculty of the will, as Arendt understood it, is unlike thinking in that it is much closer to the realm of appearances. It, together with judging, is directed at particulars.[30] Unlike *either* thinking or judging, however, willing has an active element: it is concerned with projects, not objects,[31] and for this reason enjoys a freedom that neither of the other two faculties can claim. Since its direction is always towards the future, the will in a sense represents most fully man's temporal condition. Always impatient and hopeful, the will seeks to fulfil itself in the active transformation of the world. The contrast between thinking and willing is described by Arendt in terms of different 'tonalities': 'Speaking in terms of tonality, – that is, in terms of the way the mind affects the soul and produces its *moods*, regardless of outside events, thus creating a kind of *life* of the mind – the predominant mood of the thinking ego is *serenity*, the mere enjoyment of an activity that never has to overcome the resistance of matter ... The predominant mood of the Will is *tenseness*, which brings ruin to the "mind's tranquillity." '[32]

The antagonism between thinking and willing is occasioned by the conflicting needs of man to be 'at home' with himself and the world, and his urge to be constantly overturning what is given to him for the sake of a better future. The will always seeks change, turmoil, and disruption. Its very nature is to be restless and dissatisfied. The problem for the will then, within the entire structure of the mind, is how to reconcile its restlessness with the 'stillness' of thought. Both are required for a fully human life.

According to Arendt, the faculty of the will has been systematically denied its rightful place within the tradition of thought precisely because of the difficulty that thought has in dealing with the will's contingency. Much of the volume on 'Willing' is preoccupied with showing how, in what ingenious ways, philosophers have managed to repress the will. In antiquity, philosophy was dominated by the ideal of the *bios theoretikos*, a conception of man dwelling in the neighbourhood of the everlasting; in the medieval period, the *vita contemplativa* provided the consoling thought of divine providence; and in the modern period, the will has been submerged in the *philosophy of history*.[33] We already know from Arendt's earlier writings on history and tradition how she attributed the demise of action to these dominant modes of thought. Will, in a major aspect the mental organ of action, has suffered the same fate. Will and action both have been given negligible treatment by philosophers because they belong to the realm of contingency and do not lend themselves easily to theoretical exposition.

Just as Arendt had begun her reflections on thinking by questioning anew certain prejudices within the tradition, so too in 'Willing' she began by trying to sort out the basis of recurring recriminations against the will. Is the denigration of freedom a flight from contingency caused by a fear of the unknown, or is there something integral to the structure of the mind that prevents the will from asserting itself?

Arendt looked at what she considered to be the formative descriptions of the will in pre-modern thinkers: those given by St Paul, Epictetus, and Duns Scotus. In every instance, she found that the author eventually retreated from hypostasizing the will as an independent faculty. In Paul, the will gives way to faith; in Epictetus, stoicism is the answer given to the will's futility; and in Duns Scotus the will is ultimately defeated by the law of causality. All these pre-modern thinkers found it necessary to subordinate the will to some other object, or cause, that could suppress its open-endedness. These findings did not surprise Arendt, for she anticipated that in a world dominated by a cyclical understanding of time (such as the ancients inhabited), or in one dominated by the belief in divine providence (the Christian world), the spontaneity and freedom of the intellect could not have been fully explored.

But in the waning of metaphysics and religious faith, Arendt expected that the will would have become much more significant in modern thought. With the moderns, she wrote, 'we are entitled to expect an even stronger interest in a mental organ for the future ... because the modern age's main and entirely new concept, the notion of *Progress*, as the ruling force in human history, placed an unprecedented emphasis on the future.'[34] What she was to find, to the contrary, was that the moderns, even those who began by asserting the autonomy of the will, repudiated the will even more thoroughly than their predecessors had done. Arendt singled out Hegel and Nietzsche for special consideration, since they, more than any other of the moderns, were concerned with the problem of 'becoming.'

Hegel may have started philosophizing with the emphasis on becoming rather than 'Being,' but his philosophy of history construes becoming in such a way that it is robbed of the freedom and wilfulness that human beings execute in creating a civilization. There is no need here to go into Arendt's account of Hegel's philosophy of history: her criticisms of Hegel in *The Life of the Mind* are not new. There is one point that she emphasized, however: behind all Hegel's admiration for the self-constituting process of history and his celebration of 'becoming,' lies the age-old conviction that 'being' is ultimately necessary to give meaning to human affairs. Hegel's outstanding philosophical *coup* was making 'being' appear in history by making man coeval with time. As Arendt put it: 'What in later existential thought became the notion of the auto-production of man's mind we find in Hegel as the "auto-constitution of Time": man is not just temporal; he *is* Time.'[35]

Identifying man as time is what Arendt objected to most in Hegel's thought, for it was her firm belief that man is born *into* time; he is not identical with it. Hegel tried to rescue man from his entrapment between 'being' and 'becoming' by turning 'being' into the progress of the World Spirit, but in so doing he destroyed any notion of the individual will to become. For if the tension between the past and the future is eliminated by making all time the embodiment of a single purpose, the will has no place. Indeed, it comes to rest. For Arendt, taking Hegel seriously would mean accepting the fact that human history (whose agent is the restless will) had actually come to an end. 'Philosophy in the Hegelian sense – the owl of Minerva that starts its flight at dusk – demands an arrest in real time, not merely the suspension of time during the activity of the thinking ego. In other words, Hegel's philosophy could claim objective truth only on condition that history were factually at an end, that mankind had no more future, that nothing could still occur that would bring anything new.'[36]

Turning subsequently to Nietzsche, who himself had reacted to Hegel, Arendt found that Nietzsche's thought included a repudiation of the will as absolute as Hegel's. Nietzsche began with the proposition that life is the highest value, and with the accompanying postulate that 'essence' and 'appearance' are one and the same: both reside in the living human being. Nietzsche's courage lay in his efforts to think about meaning without any of the metaphysical supports of the tradition. Initially, he rejected the transcendent measure of thought and Hegel's notion of historical progress because he wanted to assert the strength and autonomy of human will. As Arendt summarized Nietzsche's original intention: 'Nietzsche embarked on a construction of the given world that would make sense, be a fitting abode for a creature whose "strength of will" [is great enough] to do without meaning in things ... [who] can endure to live in a meaningless world.'[37]

Lamentably, Nietzsche's efforts to make the will paramount failed, and he ended up with a contrary view of things. He realized that it is impossible to assert freedom as the highest value and to reflect upon the assertion at the same time. The problem of memory obstructs the will. As soon as we reflect upon the meaning of supposedly free acts, we see that there are patterns in any chain of events that seem to preclude the possibility of freedom. We are as bound by the past as we are enticed by the possibilities for the future. According to Arendt, it was the perceived clash between past and future that 'made Nietzsche experiment with

Eternal Recurrence.'[38] Since he was bound by the past preventing him from exalting freedom, but did not want to accept Hegel's notion that all of history is the march of mankind towards some rational goal, Nietzsche saw no way out except by turning freedom into a gratuitous praise of the world as it is 'given,' eternally, to the senses. As Arendt commented: 'The "thought of Eternal Return" implies an unconditional denial of the modern rectilinear time concept and its progressing course.'[39] Yet even in denying that history moves in a progressive fashion, Nietzsche could not 'save' the will. It does, indeed, seem as if there is something in the activity of thought that prevent us from *thinking* of an autonomous will. The most eloquent expression of this truth is perhaps in Heidegger, to whom Arendt ascribed the conviction that 'To act is to err, to go astray.'[40] Heidegger came to view willing as a sort of stubborn and never-ending 'crashing' against the order of things. Unlike Nietzsche, however, he did not try to resolve this puzzling activity by annihilating the will in a conception of eternal return. Instead, he thought that the errancy of the will was a tragic disorder of the human psyche.[41] Arendt felt that Heidegger's only 'solution' to the problem of the will was resignation to the fact that a human being is doomed to be free and doomed to die at the same time. As such, he is a 'detractor' from the order of things.

Concluding her foraging through the history of thought, Arendt found not one single philosopher who was able to give a coherent account of the will. Even when she turned her attention away from philosophers to men of action, to see how the latter explained the new beginnings in the political realm, she fared no better. Looking at what she considered the two great foundation legends of Western civilization – the Roman and the Hebrew legends – Arendt discovered that both referred to a sense of willing a new community into being. In scrutinizing these legends more closely, though, one finds this sense of novelty is abandoned in the story of the founding. Both legends refer to some authoritative source outside the actual community to legitimate their new order. In the Hebrew legend, there is a Creator-God who 'can explain, give a logical account of the existentially inexplicable,'[42] and in the Roman legend, the new beginning is interpreted as the 'resurgence of Troy and the re-establishment of a city-state that had preceded Rome.'[43] One legend turned to eternity, the other to history, but both dissolved the hiatus in which a new start was made by situating it in a context of meaning that lay beyond the freely willed acts of individuals. Much more recently, in the founding of the United States, Arendt discovered the same search for accountability. The Fathers of the Republic spoke of their task as the founding of a new Rome, again recalling the past to justify the future. This profession confirmed for Arendt that the existential need for continuity and purpose is as urgent for men of action as it is for philosophers. In both cases, the need has been as great as the need for freedom. No matter how hard one might try to account for the autonomy and freedom of action 'purged of the perplexities caused for men's minds by the reflexivity of mental activities, one cannot succeed.'[44]

That the will cannot be shown to have an autonomy from the reflexivity of mental activities may, in fact, turn out to be a positive thing. As Arendt conceptualized it, the will seems to have built into it the simultaneity of 'willing' and 'nilling.' These contrary impulses of the willing faculty act as a control upon the open-endedness and caprice of freedom. Choice may need boundaries or restrictions against which it can exercise meaningful options. As Arendt put it: 'A will that would be "entire," without a counter-will, could no longer be a will properly speaking.'[45] Even though all theoretical accounts of the will seem to find the obstacles of free choice overwhelming, it would be a far graver error to assume that the will had no obstacles whatsoever. To claim that human beings are absolutely free would require that the other faculties of the mind – judging and thinking – be forcibly repressed from consciousness. To will 'out of nothing,' disregarding thought and judgment, would seem to be the source of what Arendt called the banality of evil. Though she did not make such an equation explicitly in *The Life of the Mind*, I think it can be inferred from her work as a whole, and especially from her reflections on totalitarianism.[46]

Oddly enough, though Arendt found no evidence of the will's autonomy either in the history of thought or in the accounts given of the foundings of regimes, she did not consider the prominent role that willing played in the totalitarian movements of the twentieth century. Totalitarian states seem to be an obvious example of regimes that feel no need to ground their legitimacy in the judgment of the past, or in any transcendent measure of thought. As Arendt herself said, the 'principle' of totalitarian states is 'sheer movement.' To make perpetual movement, rather than stability, the motivating principle of politics is to transgress the 'natural' order of things, as Arendt warned in *The Origins of Totalitarianism*. Totalitarian regimes can be seen as the only instance in which freedom has been truly made the highest value, unencumbered by the reservations of thought and judgment. They claim that man can be made over into anything he wishes to become; their objective is 'to make mankind itself the embodiment of the law.'[47] The will that is required to actualize such a project is one that does not heed the contradictions within itself: it does not 'hear' the 'nilling' that is the proper restriction of action. When human beings think that they can fashion themselves and the world in any manner they wish, they are able to do so only for as long as they can keep the other faculties of the mind in abeyance. The latter *can* be done, as Arendt demonstrated in her work on totalitarianism, through a combination of ideology and terror.

But a person who wills without qualification does not heed his own 'conscience'; he wills without thinking and, in so doing, goes contrary to his own nature. That such distortion of the life of the mind is possible Arendt did not doubt, but those who engage in it are not 'fully human.' The sad proof of the kind of havoc that unbridled 'willing' can wreak upon civilization is found in the consequences of totalitarian rule. 'Until now, the totalitarian belief that everything is possible seems to have proved only that everything can be destroyed.'[48]

What the study of totalitarian regimes ought to tell us is that the will is not and should not be thought of as autonomous. The will's drive towards the future and its insatiable desire to master contingency can never be gratified, for its gratification means the distortion of the human condition. I think Arendt realized at the end of 'Willing' that philosophers have understandably shirked the will because they recognized the dangers within it.

The philosopher to whom Arendt appealed at the end of 'Willing' was Augustine: the thinker who had first conceived of the will as a faculty divided against itself. For Augustine, it was in the 'nature' of the will to command obedience, but also to resist its own commands. In resolving this impasse, Augustine did not recommend annihilating the will or suppressing the resistance to it but, rather, he called upon the healing power of love to mitigate the will's contradictions. Whatever Augustine may have meant by the healing power of love, Arendt interpreted it to mean a kind of thinking. She wrote: 'The emphasis ... is on the mind *thinking* of itself, and the love that stills the will's turmoil and restlessness is not a love of tangible things but of the "footprints," "sensible things" have left on the inwardness of the mind.'[49]

Hence, willing points the way back to thinking as its grounding principle. The 'awesome responsibility' of freedom is met by the reference to other faculties of the mind. Of particular importance in settling the disquietude of the will is the faculty of judgment, for it is this memory-faculty that leaves the so-called footprints on the mind.

Judging

It is not certain what the third faculty of the mind would have looked like had Arendt lived to complete the volume. As her friend and executor Mary McCarthy wrote in the postface to *The Life of the Mind*, 'anyone familiar with her mind will feel sure' that what we have in the way of thoughts on judging 'do not exhaust the ideas that must already have been stirring in her head as she inserted the fresh page in her typewriter.'[50] In fact, there is not always a continuity between the remarks that Arendt made about judging in the two completed volumes of *The Life of the Mind* and what she wrote in the lectures on Kant's political philosophy, though the Kant lectures have been regarded by many as the basic groundwork for 'Judging.' I will consider both the context of 'Thinking' and 'Willing' and the Kant lectures to elucidate what I think constituted Hannah Arendt's theory of judging.

Arendt concluded her study of 'Willing' by opening up an inquiry into another faculty, judging; the reasons for this are apparent. We know that she surmised that the will, to be meaningful, had to have within itself a 'counter-will.' Also, in keeping with the elaborate metaphor of consciousness drawn in 'Thinking,' we know that each of the faculties was associated by her with a 'time sense'; within the order of the mind, each of the time dimensions performs a balancing function for the others. Judgment clearly, for her, was the faculty that represents the memory of the past: judging occurs when 'I transcend the limits of my own life span and begin to reflect on the past.'[51] Recollection of the past and collecting things into the memory for consideration by the mind as a whole have particular significance for the will, because no one ought to will in a vacuum. The 'footprints left on the mind' to which Arendt alluded at the end of 'Willing' are there by virtue of judgment. Unlike the products of thinking that are always opaque and elusive, judging produces particulars to consciousness. Judging is much more of a historically sensitive faculty than thinking in this respect; it takes its examples from that which is manifest in the world. As Arendt put it: 'The faculty of judging particulars (as brought to light by Kant), the ability to say "this is wrong," "this is beautiful," and so on, is not the same as the faculty of thinking. Thinking deals with invisibles, with representations of things that are absent; judging always concerns particulars.'[52]

Yet, Arendt seemed to understand judging as a 'by-product' of thinking. Even though judging always draws on particulars, the discrimination among the things we choose to remember is not determined simply by what the world offers to us. There is an interchange between thinking and judging that sensitizes us to appreciate certain things. Thinking prepares the mind for making good judgments and judging, in turn, gives worldly content to the 'nowhere' of thought. Arendt expressed the interchange between thinking and judging as follows: 'If thinking – the two-in-one of the soundless dialogue – actualizes the difference within our identity as given in consciousness and thereby results in conscience as its by-product, then judging, the by-product of the liberating effect of thinking, realizes thinking, makes it manifest in the world of appearances where I am never alone and always too busy to be able to think.'[53]

The relationship between thinking and judging would have been of overriding importance for Arendt, I think, because judgment on its own can present distortions of the mind similar to those that are caused by excessive 'willing.' Dwelling on the past can have a crippling effect on the capacity to act. From Arendt's writings throughout her life, we have her lamentations on philosophers who have been too much preoccupied with extracting meaning from the past. We saw, in 'Willing,' how she singled out Hegel and Nietzsche as modern philosophers who 'succumbed' to the past, forgoing the idea of free will. In contrast to the great modern philosophers of history for whom history held its own, integral meaning, Arendt thought that judgment was a task performed by living, distinct individuals. This is why the spectator held a special place in her thought. The spectator is not a philosopher of history; he does not seek patterns or meaning or progress as in the backward glance of the historian. He takes a dispassionate interest in the haphazard wealth of phenomena that appears in the world, acknowledging the importance of the ugly as well as the beautiful, the foolish as well as the noble. The special gift of the spectator is 'taste,' and Arendt hoped that taste would be able to win back human dignity 'from the pseudo-divinity named history.' Unfortunately, there is no elaboration at all on the role of taste in the faculty of judgment in the existing pages of *The Life of the Mind*. For an indication of this role, we have to turn to the lectures on Kant's political philosophy.

In the Kant lectures, Arendt situated 'taste' squarely between willing and judging as the capacity, or sense, that keeps these two faculties in a proper balance with one another. According to her, Kant was fully aware of the inherent contradiction between the standpoint of the spectator-judge and that of the actor. This is manifest in his contradictory attitudes towards the French Revolution. From the standpoint of action, Kant could applaud events of the revolution since they signified the glory of human choice, but from the standpoint of the spectator, who judges historical events according to the contribution they make to universal peace, Kant condemned the immoderation of revolutionary acts. To Arendt, Kant's views on the French Revolution represented 'a clash between the principle according to which you should act and the principle according to which you judge.'[54] Arendt did not think that this clash was nonsensical, but rather that it was something inherent within the human condition itself. The problem, as she saw it, was: How do we preserve both action and judgment in their autonomy and still make sense of human existence? She admired Kant's steadfastness in the face of such tensions. In his efforts to preserve both the integrity of free action and the need for judgment, Kant avoided the excesses of too great a faith in progress and too melancholy a resignation to the fate of history. In Arendt's view, it was because of the contradictions of Kant's position that he avoided becoming either an 'idealistic fool' or a 'criminal.'[55]

Kant used taste as a concept to bridge the gap between wilful action and judgment. Taste allows us to be pleased or displeased with something, independent of moral considerations. Things and events in the world can please us and fill us with awe and admiration, even though they have no meaning or may be immoral. Kant could be pleased at the spectacle of the French Revolution, though when he brought moral considerations to bear on his judgment, he was appalled at the violence and disruption that it caused. It is necessary, thought Kant, to retain both the aesthetic element of taste and the moral sensibility in one's mind simultaneously. As Arendt said, since in matters of taste 'there can be no dispute about right and wrong,'[56] taste has to be moderated by some guiding principle. In the Kant lectures, two such moderating principles are mentioned: common sense and imagination. These are the factors that circumscribe taste and give it substantive content.

Common sense directs the immediacy of taste (the subjective 'it pleases me') back to the world of shared experience, in much the same way as the association of thinking with metaphor directs the subjectivity of thinking back to the world of shared language. Taste, for Kant, has a cultural affinity in that tastes are cultivated in society with other human beings. Common sense supposedly informs our tastes by bringing them into accord with the tastes of others. Arendt put it this way: 'As for common sense: Kant was very early aware that there was something non-subjective in what seems to be the most private and subjective sense ... "We are ashamed if our taste does not agree with others." '[57]

The 'worldliness' of common sense accounts for how taste builds cultures. Our judgments of the world are, at least in some respects, reflections of our historical place and our cultural prejudices. The relative homogeneity of taste in any culture indicates how important the whole matter of public opinion is to judgment. The cultural particularity of judgment was important to Arendt (and presumably to Kant) because, as Ronald Beiner states in his critical essay on Arendt's Kant lectures, it emphasizes the significance of opinion in political and social life: 'It is clear that judgment and opinion belong inextricably together as the chief faculties of political reason. Arendt's intention is fairly obvious: to concentrate attention on the faculty of judgment is to rescue opinion from the disrepute into which it has fallen since Plato. Both faculties, that of judging and that of forming opinions, are thus redeemed simultaneously.'[58]

But opinion *cannot* be the sole, or even the most important, basis for judgment. The association of judgment with public opinion was surely one of the things that concerned Arendt most, in light of her observations on Eichmann. Though judgment belongs 'in the world,' and certainly in many instances reflects the consensus of community opinion, the individual must be capable of formulating judgments independent of the prevailing opinions around him, especially, as Arendt said, in critical situations where individual judgment has grave consequences. That which ultimately overrules consensus and common sense as the basis of judgment in Kant's philosophy is imagination. 'Private conditions condition us; imagination and reflection enable us to liberate ourselves from them and to attain that relative impartiality that is the specific virtue of judgment.'[59]

The imagination is able to present to the individual the idea of mankind, that is, a general principle of mankind that is not spatially or temporally limited. It is thus distinct from common sense, which is the embodiment of a specific community of historically based opinions. Imagination in effect carries the particularity of cultural taste over into a comparison with a general principle that is supplied not through observation of the world or through common-sense observations, but through thinking. Arendt stated emphatically that good judgment is intrinsically tied to the generality of thinking. In the Kant lectures, she actually called judging the combination of assessing particulars and thinking: 'The chief difficulty in judgment is that it is "the faculty of thinking the particular" but to *think* means to generalize, hence, it is the faculty of mysteriously combining the particular and the general ... I cannot judge one particular by another particular; in order to determine its worth, I need a *tertium quid* or a *tertium comparationis*, something related to the particular and yet distinct from both.'[60]

In the lectures, Arendt noted that Kant had subsumed both the imagination and the capacity for evaluating particulars under the overarching concept of judgment. She found this problematic and speculated that what Kant called the imaginative part of judging actually belonged to another faculty: 'What Kant calls the faculty of the imagination, to make present to the mind what is absent from sense perception, has less to do with memory than with another faculty, one that has been known since the beginnings of philosophy ... Parmenides (fragment 4) called it *nous*.'[61] This 'other faculty,' though unnamed in the Kant lectures, is evidently what Arendt later came to call 'thinking' when she wrote *The Life of the Mind*. Everything Arendt said about Kant's concept of the imagination – that it is 'the *condition* for memory,' that 'it does not need to be led by temporal associations' but 'can make present at will what it chooses,' that it is a 'blind but indispensable function of the soul' – is in accord with what she said about thinking in volume one of *The Life of the Mind*.

I think it is likely that the lectures that Arendt delivered on Kant's philosophy in the late 1960s were instrumental in setting the context for her final project on the life of the mind. The reflections upon common sense, taste, and imagination remain dominant themes in 'Thinking' and 'Willing.' But I do not think that Arendt ascribed the same qualities to these things as did Kant. Common sense remains an integral part of judging, but not the most important factor. Taste is superseded by imaginative thinking: it is thinking that prepares the way for making judgments. Had Arendt completed the projected volume on 'Judging,' I think it would have taken its place as an equal partner with 'Willing' in the life of the mind. As a faculty oriented towards the past and towards particular recollections, it is limited in its capacity to account for human experience. Judgment does not contain within itself either the freedom to will or the freedom to think. What it can do is present particular events and deeds of exemplary validity that give content to the winds of thought and a cautionary check upon the impatience of the will. The supposed impasse posed by willing – that we 'will' and 'nill' at the same time – appears less problematic when we consider willing together with judging, for will must give way as it were to the equal need of judgment. That judging and willing can each hold its place within the life of the mind, contradicting yet complementing one another, we owe to the third faculty: thinking. Only by abstracting from 'this particular act of will' or 'this particular judgment' can we avoid the imperative voices of the future and the past and view them instead as constituent parts of mental life.

The Republic of Faculties

Commentary on *The Life of the Mind* has been sparse and tentative, probably because of the unfinished nature of the work. Interestingly, what has aroused the most interest is the unwritten finale on judging. There has been much speculation on what the last volume would have said and some have contended that this would have been the pinnacle of Arendt's work, the thing that would have contained her last word on the life of the mind, and would have resolved any contradictions in her thought. Ronald Beiner, for example, has written: 'For Arendt, the act of judging represents the culmination of the tripartite activity of the mind because, on the one hand, it maintains the contact with "the world of appearances" that is characteristic of "willing", and, on the other hand it fulfills the quest for meaning that animates "thinking." '[62]

It is understandable how judging could be seen to be the crowning achievement of Arendt's inquiry into the mental processes, given the import that she had placed upon the role of the spectator in history. In the essay on 'The Crisis in Culture,' we recall the admiration that Arendt exprerssed for the 'humanist' who, because 'he is not a specialist, exhibits a faculty of judgment and taste which is beyond the coercion which each specialty imposes upon us.' The outstanding characteristic of the spectator-humanist, according to Arendt in this essay, is 'an attitude that knows how to take care and preserve and admire the things of the world.'[63] In her essays on select individuals in *Men in Dark Times* Arendt singled out the capacity for 'judging' or 'disinterested spectatorship' as the specific talent of some of these figures. Of Karl Jaspers she wrote that he had in his character the *humanitas* of one who possesses unfailingly good judgment. Thought of the sort practised by Jaspers 'is bound to be political even when it deals with things that are not in the least political; for it always confirms that Kantian "enlarged mentality" which is the political mentality *par excellence*.'[64] And in perhaps her strongest affirmation of the importance of judging, Arendt had this to say in reference to the great story-teller Isak Dinesen: 'It is true that storytelling reveals meaning without committing the error of defining it, that it brings about consent and reconciliation with things as they really are, and that we may even trust it to contain eventually by implication the last word which we expect from the "day of judgment." '[65]

The notion that judgment is intended to reconcile human beings to things as they are is elaborated by Ronald Beiner; he regards this as the primary characteristic not only of judging, but of Arendt's thought as a whole. To this end, he sees Arendt's theory of judgment as being a tragic conception of human existence: 'Human judgment tends to be tragic judgment. It continually confronts a reality that it can never fully master but to which it must none the less reconcile itself.'[66] I do not believe that this was Arendt's last word on the human condition. She was vociferously opposed to the idea that we can reconcile the tensions in existence by resolving them in thought. Beiner draws an explicit comparison between Arendt and Nietzsche: 'The path of reflection that led Arendt to consider the faculty of judging runs parallel to that which led Nietzsche to posit the eternal return.'[67] Yet Arendt resisted Nietzsche's resignation to the past; she thought it an inadequate response to the difficulties of the will; in her understanding of Nietzsche, his 'last word' on the subject of willing 'clearly spells a repudiation of the Will and the willing ego.'[68] She was not willing to abandon the notion of free will for anything like Nietzsche's reconciliation to the past.

Not tragedy, but hope, is the persistent mood of the life of the mind. Despite so many theoretical obstacles, Arendt insisted upon the freedom of both thinking and willing. Beiner's comment that 'Arendt looked to judging as the only way out of the impasse' posed by the volume on willing seems to accord judging an *Aufhebung* that was not part of Arendt's project.[69] If nothing else, her lifelong commitment to action should tell us that she did not suddenly give up this preoccupation in her last work for the quietistic activity of judging. Moreover, when Arendt began her inquiry into the life of the mind, she was thinking about the consequences that thinking and judging have for acting in the world. Since judging is always about particulars, it has meaning for the individual living in a particular present, and has a direct bearing on the direction of the will. But, according to Beiner, judging became the substitute for acting in Arendt's final work; he sees it as a last attempt on Arendt's part to salvage human dignity from a tragic course of affairs:

> There is only the remotest possibility of deriving a sense of meaning from action in the present. (In these circumstances – in a world where the possibility of acting politically is more or less foreclosed – judging almost becomes a kind of vicarious action, a way of recouping our citizenship in default of a genuine public realm.) Nor is there any more reason to expect meaningfulness to be secured by willing projects or by projecting our will into the future (hence the impasse with respect to willing). That leaves the faculty of judgment, which can at least locate past events that redeem human existence.[70]

Without wanting to demean the role of judging in Arendt's thought – it clearly was one of the things with which she was most preoccupied – I think it is incorrect to place it at the centre of her concerns in *The Life of the Mind*. To do so contradicts Arendt's own contention in 'Thinking' that human beings can transcend the conditions of their particular circumstances by virtue of all three faculties: 'They can judge affirmatively or negatively the realities they are born into and by which they are also conditioned; they can will the impossible, for instance eternal life; and they can think, that is, speculate meaningfully about the unknown and the unknowable.'[71] An overemphasis on judging discredits the integrity of the other faculties.

In addition, as I inferred earlier, I don't see how it would be possible to have a meaningful theory of judgment that is divorced from a theory of the will. It may be difficult, as Beiner commented, 'to derive a sense of meaning from action in the present' if we mean by action the creation of public spaces of the sort that Arendt had described in *The Human Condition*, but our times, perhaps *more* than others, demand that individuals exhibit a will to act differently from the majority of people around them. What Arendt demanded of Eichmann, for example, was not simply that he be able to judge, but that he act on the basis of those judgments in a morally responsible way. There are some radical situations in which action, or active resistance, is mandatory, and the best judgment under such circumstances is useless unless it is transformed into a will *not* to let things rest as they are. In radical situations, all the faculties of the mind are brought together in a single response; thinking liberates judgment and judgment is transformed into wilful resistance: 'When everybody is swept away unthinkingly by what everybody else does and believes in, those who think are drawn out of hiding because their refusal to join in is conspicuous and thereby becomes a kind of action.'[72]

Another commentator on *The Life of the Mind*, Barry Clarke, has emphasized the bond between judgment and will and points out that Eichmann's failure to judge cannot be attributed to anything like bad memory or faulty mental capacities. He did not judge because he was *unwilling* to summon his mental capacities: In the case of Eichmann, 'his value to his masters was based not on his *inability* to use his own reflective judgment, but on his *willingness* not to bring the faculties of his mind to bear on his task.'[73]

In emphasizing the will in connection with judgment, I think Clarke comes closer to an appreciation of what Arendt was trying to accomplish. It is the inherent freedom of the mind that she wanted to prove, a freedom that can survive even in the midst of the most unfree political conditions. Judgment as reconciliation to the past is transcended within the entire structure of the mind by those aspects of thinking that resist reconciliation. Thinking accomplishes this end by reaching out beyond the limits of particular knowledge, and willing does it by its stubborn confidence in the possibilities for a better world. The three faculties together, as indicated in the prefatory remarks to this chapter, constitute the true realm of freedom in which it is possible to make choices in the present that are determined neither by what has gone before nor by some sweeping project for the future. This freedom of the mind is the condition for our capacity to act morally, and for our 'right' to judge others. In refusing the 'gift' of freedom that is the prerogative of every thinking human being, Eichmann denied his 'essence.' As Clarke put it, the great evil of Eichmann is that he chose not to choose: 'It is because Eichmann failed at a time of great crisis to do other than continue in obedience to his superiors, because he abnegated his own judgment, thought and will, that he can be said to have chosen choicelessness.'[74]

The demarcating quality of the life of the mind in its entirety is its freedom. Thinking, willing, and judging together form what Elisabeth Young-Bruehl has aptly termed a kind of 'mental republic' that exists potentially in every human being simply by virtue of his having been born.[75] When political freedom is absent from the world, this freedom of the mind can survive. Though it takes an exemplary individual to sustain freedom under such unpropitious circumstances, it is to this extraordinary individual that we must look for guidance. Karl Jaspers was, for Arendt, such an individual, as we have noted before: 'What Karl Jaspers represented ... when he was entirely alone, was not Germany but what was left of *humanitas* in Germany. It was as if he alone in his inviolability could illuminate that space which reason creates and preserves between men, and as if the light and breadth of this space would survive even if only one man were to remain in it.'[76]

Not that this 'inviolability' of the life of the mind can ever substitute for the enjoyment of freedom in the public realm, but in dark times it can none the less keep freedom alive and sustain the hope that freedom in the world is a real possibility as long as there are living human beings.[77] The best, most succinct summary of Hannah Arendt's intent in *The Life of the Mind* comes from her student and biographer, Elisabeth Young-Bruehl: 'What she did, in *The Life of the Mind*, was to show how a philosophical investigation of the Mind can offer political theory a portrait of the thinking, willing and judging faculties *in their freedom*. When, in the political realm, there is no freedom for the manifestations of will and judgment, acting and speaking your judgments, the wonder is that the mind can still be active. Were it not able to be free *in itself*, this would not be so.'[78]

Freedom is the quality that best characterizes the life of the mind as a whole, but it is obvious that freedom cannot reign in the mind of a time-bound individual unless he 'stops to think.' When the gift of thinking is refused, judgment and will are corrupted. That the gift of thinking *can* be refused is testimony to the 'awesome responsibility' of the human condition. In the end, I believe Arendt remained firm in her conviction that sane thought is something that we can demand from every sane person, and towards that objective we have a responsibility to create conditions under which the exercise of free thought is encouraged. As a teacher, this is all Arendt tried to do. As a person concerned about the fate of the world, she felt that thinking was by implication political, since it is by thinking critically about things that people are able to alter existing conditions. The priority that she placed upon thinking is evident in a response she gave to Christian Bay at a conference held on her work at York University in Toronto. Bay asked: 'Hannah Arendt, what can we as political theorists do to see that the existential issues – which sometimes have true and false answers – are brought home to more of our fellow citizens?' Arendt replied at length:

> I cannot tell you, black on white – and would hate to do it – what the consequences of the kind of thought I try, not to indoctrinate, but to rouse or awaken in my students, are in actual politics. I can very well imagine that one becomes a republican, and the third becomes a liberal or God knows what. But one thing I would hope: that certain extreme things which are the actual consequences of non-thinking, that is, of somebody who really has decided that he does not want to do (i.e., to think) what I do perhaps excessively, that he doesn't want to do it at all – that these consequences will not be capable [of arising]. That is, when the chips are down, the question is how will they act. And then this notion that I examine my assumptions, that I think ... that I think 'critically,' and that I don't let myself get away with repeating the cliches of the public mood [comes into play]. And I would say that any society that has lost respect for this, is not in very good shape.[79]

5 The *Vita Contemplativa* and Political Responsibility

The final evaluative considerations in this study of Hannah Arendt's thought will take stock of the dramatic shift in Arendt's emphasis on the life of the mind in the latter part of her intellectual development. Two important questions have to be raised: (1) Does her understanding of the relationship between action and thought make sense? and (2) What are the ramifications of this understanding for political action? Before addressing these matters,however, a brief summary of the major changes in her thought is in order.

Summary

Arendt began her inquiry into the stature of the human condition with a concern for two things: to discover the permanent capacities of the human being, and to demonstrate that, contrary to the central tenet of Western philosophy, action –not thought – is the apex of human endeavour and achievement. The project, as she soon discovered, was a formidable one for it involved taking account of a complex and well-entrenched tradition of thought. The difficulty was compounded by the fact that in rejecting the tradition, Arendt had to formulate new categories for thinking about the world. In *The Human Condition* we have the best example of the originality of her mind; her conceptualization of labour, work, and action as the constituent elements of individual existence are highly unorthodox, but compelling.

Arendt ranked the three activities of the *vita activa* in a number of different ways. From the standpoint of the sheer preservation of the species, labour is the most important. Without the continual regeneration and provision of life, and the collaboration of all human beings in this basic human activity, none of the other activities of the human condition would be possible. But from the standpoint of what Arendt called 'worldliness' – that is, from an appreciation of an objectified world of human artifice – work is the most significant activity. It is work that detaches man from his immediate dependence upon nature and from his subjection to the repetitive cycles of labour, and allows him to build a distinctly human world. Work's capacity to reify and objectify distinguishes the particular human being from his collective being as part of the species. Looked at from the viewpoint of this capacity for distinction and individuality, work is superior to labour. From yet a third perspective – that of plurality and freedom – action is paramount. It is only in action that human beings exhibit their capacity for joining together, voluntarily, for the purpose of creating a community in which individuals can distinguish themselves in word and deed.

We can see from Arendt's analysis that the ranking order of the activities of the *vita activa* is ambiguous. Depending upon the primacy that is ascribed to any particular 'value' –life itself, 'worldliness,' or freedom and plurality – a different activity will appear at the top of the hierarchy. However, in general, Arendt ordered the activities of the *vita activa* according to the twofold criteria of freedom and plurality. Action clearly ranks first in this case. With respect to the criterion of freedom, Arendt wrote: 'Of the three [activities] action has the closest connection with the human condition of natality: the new beginning inherent in birth can make itself felt in the world only because the newcomer possesses the capacity of beginning something anew, that is, of acting.'[1] And with respect to the criterion of plurality, Arendt stated that 'action ... corresponds to the human condition of plurality, to the fact that men, not Man, live on the earth and inhabit the world.'[2]

The ranking of work and labour, relative to action, is less clear, but applying the same criteria – freedom and plurality – it seems that Arendt placed work above labour in the hierarchy. Work is certainly secondary to action in its potential to embody freedom, because the activity of work is limited by its subordination to use value. Work, unlike action, is not freely chosen for its own sake: 'The actual work of fabrication is performed under the guidance of a model in accordance with which the object is constructed.'[3] Work is superior to labour, however, because while *homo faber* is a 'solitary' individual, whose overriding characteristic is his ability to objectify and distinguish individual existence, he is able to constitute as 'public realm' of sorts in the form of a market-place where work-objects are exchanged. The realm of *homo faber* is partially successful in creating a community: 'Unlike the *animal laborans*, whose social life is worldless and herdlike and who therefore is incapable of building or inhabiting a public, worldly realm, *homo faber* is fully capable of having a public realm of his own, even though it may not be a political realm, properly speaking.'[4] Work ranks second in the ordering of the *vita activa*; even though it fails to meet the criterion of freedom, it partially meets the criterion of plurality.

Labour has neither freedom nor plurality as constituent elements of its activity. Arendt was emphatic that labour is 'forced upon us by necessity,'[5] that *animal laborans* is 'driven by the needs of its body.'[6] Labour was, for Arendt, the most unfree of all human activities. Although labour is, by definition, the primal thing that all human beings share in common (all human beings are driven by the same basic needs), Arendt did not regard this human collectivity as anything like what she called human 'plurality.' Plurality, as was noted, was defined by her as corresponding to the condition that 'men, not Man, inhabit the world,' but by this she did not mean that plurality is equal to 'the many.' More than that, 'plurality is the condition of human action because we are all the same, that is, human, in such a way that nobody is ever the same as anyone else who ever lived, lives, or will live.'[7] In other words, plurality describes the kind of unity in which diversity and idividualism is possible. According to Arendt, labour is an activity in which all human beings are unified, but it is the *one* activity in which individuation is impossible. This distinction between unity (or collectivity) and plurality is manifest in Arendt's comments about the division of labour in society. Even in the diversification of labour, Arendt claimed that this diversity did not, and could not, constitute 'plurality,' for it is precisely the division of *labour* that is the decisive factor. The actual human beings are completely interchangeable and replaceable. 'Division of labour is based on the fact that two men can put their labour power together and "behave toward each other as though they were one." This one-ness is the exact opposite of cooperation, it indicates the unity of the species, with regard to which every single member is the same and exchangeable.'[8] Labour, then, for Arendt, occupies the lowest place in the hierarchy of the *vita activa* because it lacks *both* freedom and plurality. Action occupies the highest place: 'Action alone is the exclusive prerogative of man; neither a beast nor a god is capable of it, and only action is entirely dependent upon the constant presence of others.'[9]

Despite the innovative schematic of *The Human Condition*, Arendt's conceptualization is a problematic one. The systematic thrust of the book is twofold: it produces a rank-order of the elements belonging to the *vita activa*, as just outlined, and it subordinates the contemplative life to the active life in general. Most important for the concerns of this work was Arendt's general exaltation of action. Her efforts in *The Human Condition* were concentrated on showing how action has been denigrated in the hands of philosophers and destroyed in the practice of modern society. Action, as she understood it, has not been well regarded either by theorists (who find it too capricious) or by participants in politics (who seem to preoccupy themselves with the business of sustaining or improving life). In fact, there are hardly any instances in the entire course of history to which Arendt could point as examples of the proper ordering of action, work, and labour. This poses a tremendous problem for her whole conception, for if action constitutes the real meaning of the human condition, but action as such is practically never fulfilled, our undersanding of the human condition is severely limited. But Arendt surprised us at the end of *The Human Condition* by saying that the *truest* forms of action in the modern world may be the activities of the artist and the scientist, both of whom engage in solitary pursuits. This statement is embellished with a quotation from Cato, whose message defies the content of the rest of the book. How right Cato was, Arendt wrote, when he said: 'Never is he more active than when he does nothing; never is he less alone than when he is by himself.' This enigmatic *non sequitur* at the end of *The Human Condition* makes sense only from the perspective of Arendt's later writings.

The startling contrast between the argument of *The Human Condition* and its conclusion set the tone for all Arendt's subsequent writings. She had a commitment to action, plurality, and communication as the ground of all meaning, yet she was a philosopher in the most traditional sense: her own activity consisted in thinking and writing, and this is certainly something she accomplished by herself, in solitude. It is from this stance as a thinker, and not as an active participant in the affairs of the world, that she made these assertions.

We found that these tensions in Arendt's work are sharpened, not diminished, as her work progressed. Though she wrote prolifically about political action, both seeking its moments of glory in the great revolutions of the modern period and attempting to comprehend its grave corruption in the emergence of the totalitarian state, she consistently confronted the obstacle of thought. She feared that the total perversion of action in a totalitarian state threatened to annihilate the essential capacities of the human condition, but at the same time she praised individuals for their ability to sustain 'humanity' in their thoughts, in the absence of any 'space' for shared public action and speech. She praised the attempts to recoup action in various revolutionary movements, but showed how they repeatedly failed to achieve this objective. The failure of action to fulfil its highest potential was not attributable simply to the failures of specific situations. As she gathered together her thoughts on revolutions, Arendt realized that there appear always to be impediments to emancipatory action. These impediments are not overtly coercive. They represent an internal coercion, made possible by the inability or unwilling-ness of people to think.

The tensions in Arendt's thought remain until she reported for the *New Yorker* on the trial of Adolf Eichmann. It was at this time that she drew some definite conclusions that diverge from her arguments in *The Human Condition*. The lack of a public space and the absence of true action in a given situation do not prevent one from making meaningful judgments about the world, nor ought they to excuse one who makes bad judgments. From there, Arendt was led to say that what sustains the human condition, that is, the traditional capacities of human beings to behave with dignity and responsibility, has to be something other than the nature of the community in which an individual finds himself. These capacities have to be rooted in the existential fact of the individual. Finally, with her observations on Eichmann, Arendt came back to consider seriously Cato's proposition that man is most active when he is by himself.

Arendt's final project, *The Life of the Mind*, is an examination of the solitary activity of thinking. Arendt had clearly shifted away from her premise in *The Human Condition* – that *action* in the plural is the sine qua non and the apex of the human condition. In the preceding chapter, we found her notion of thinking to be just as unconventional and problematic as her thoughts on action. She never renounced her commitment to the affairs of the world for a notion of detached or disembodied reason. To the end of her life, she rejected metaphysics as a formalistic and false account of the thinking activity. Nor did she abandon her focus on contingency and diversity for a systematic philosophy of history. What she tried to do instead was to give an explanation of thinking that would allow for the possibility of freedom in the individual and in political communities, but would also provide criteria for making responsible, moral judgments about action. This viewpoint required a type of thinking that does not make truth claims, but that nevertheless refers to some object of responsibility. Arendt's breakdown of the structure of the mind into separate, but interdependent, faculties was a way of creating a bridge between the world of appearances (the world in which we labour, work, act, and die) and the world of thought (the realm in which we seem to withdraw from the conditions that define our possibilities for acting).

From Action to Theory

It is now possible to assess Arendt's work as a whole. The first of our critical queries can be formulated as follows: Do Arendt's various approaches to the relationship between thought and action make sense? There are really two dimensions to the question: (1) Was the shift from the primacy of action to the primacy of thought justified? In other words, was the shift to the life of the mind logically necessary; was it a step towards greater theoretical consistency? (2) Does her conception of thinking make sense?

With respect to the first dimension – Was the shift justified? – there is little doubt that to many critics Arendt's return to 'thinking' represented an anticlimax in her intellectual life. Her study of *The Life of the Mind* has not aroused the interest or the controversy of her earlier works. Ronald Beiner, for example, in writing about Arendt's theory of judgment, expresses regret that in *The Life of the Mind* Arendt was 'forced to expel judging from the world of the *vita activa*, to which it maintains a natural affinity.' The consequence of Arendt's more systematic reflections, says Beiner, is 'a much narrower (and perhaps less rich) concept of judgment.'[10] Contrary to this verdict, I would argue that Arendt's shift from the *vita activa* to the *vita contemplativa* was initiated by the theoretical impossibility of constituting meaning in terms of action alone. I also disagree with those who would claim that this shift resulted in a less rich or less illuminating understanding of the human condition. The movement from the *vita activa* to the *vita contemplativa*, I hold, was necessitated by the very nature of inquiry. Arendt realized, reluctantly, that one cannot uphold action as the sole generator of meaning, for doing so renders judgment impossible. In asserting that action is the highest and most formative activity of human life, we would have to concede that all thought is 'afterthought' and that we can judge only the consequences of action, not its designs, aims, or intentions. In other words, judgment would be rendered impotent to affect action in any way; it would be reduced to fond memories or guilty regrets. If we were to accept that unpremeditated action is the mainspring of history, how could we demand responsibility from individual actors? These are the difficulties that Arendt faced, and the gravity of them forced her to reconsider the relationship between thought and action.

The objection has been raised that even though 'free' action in the way Arendt presented it in *The Human Condition* cannot be constitutive of meaning, Arendt need not, and should not, have turned her back on the realm of political, plural activity to focus upon the mental processes of the individual. It is suggested by Habermas, for instance, that Arendt might have conceived of action differently had she not held fast to the classical distinction between theory and practice: 'An antiquated concept of theoretical knowledge that is based on ultimate insights and certainties keeps Arendt from comprehending the process of reaching agreement about practical questions as rational discourse.'[11] That is, in assuming that theory rests upon certain knowledge, and that practice (action) rests upon opinion, and in assuming further that there can be no free action where theoretical knowledge is brought to bear on political questions, Arendt put herself in an unnecessary dichotomy. She wanted to defend the freedom inherent in the opinion-oriented, relativistic political realm from the absolute judgments of 'truth-tellers,' but ultimately she concluded that a freedom untainted by theoretical maxims was not only dangerous, but meaningless. Habermas concludes: 'Arendt sees a yawning abyss between knowledge and opinion that cannot be closed with arguments.'[12]

I do not think that the 'abyss' was as cavernous as Habermas describes it, but I will pursue this point later. Currently, what concerns us is Habermas's own notion of how action can generate meaning. He contends that it is possible to adopt a critical standard for action that is not drawn from the coercive logic of theoretical truth, that is, one that is not dependent upon some objective exposition of the mental faculties, but that nevertheless is able 'to distinguish between illusory and non-illusory convictions.'[13] For Habermas, it is possible to conceive action as free, communicative, and creative and *also* as being guided by some critical standard of judgment, without thereby subordinating action to theoretical imperatives. The first step towards achieving this goal would be to eliminate the structural blockages of free communication – such obstacles as the economic structure of modern society, the institutionalization of power, and ideological propaganda. Assuming for the moment that these structural inhibitions could be eliminated, what would emerge from the communication and opinions of 'free' people? Habermas assumes that a genuine basis of common, rational meaning would emerge from such a community.

The notion that in a truly free society, unhampered by the structures of political and economic monopoly of power, a coherent and public meaning would arise does not make sense. There is too little evidence, historically or logically, that this would happen. I think Arendt realized this fact and thus did not focus her attention on how we could 'cure' modern society in such a way as to unleash freedom. She realized that even if, hypothetically, we could rid ourselves of the structural constraints upon freedom, we still would not be able to render judgments about political life without giving an account of them, and this activity involves an inquiry into the nature of theoretical judgment. Opinion, even unobstructed opinion, for her is incapable of generating meaningful action unless it is reflective and responsible, that is, unless it can give an account of the validity of its claims.

The pivotal difference between Arendt and Habermas can be formulated as follows. Habermas aims for a synthesis of theory and practice in his conceptualization of communicatively shared discourse. He holds that this discourse, carried on under unobstructed conditions, ought to be able to generate a consensus on questions of morality. This consensus, in turn, can be validated by the rational norms that are themselves supplied by intersubjectivity. Ronald Beiner summarizes Habermas's position succinctly: 'Habermas seeks to defend a cognitivist account of practical questions which upholds the truth of norms arrived at by argumentation supported by reasons. By truth is meant a consensus of rational subjects established through free and unconstrained communication.'[14]

Arendt, like Habermas, rejected the notion that truth claims have any grounding in a transcendent 'reality' that is independent of human existence among one's fellows. Unlike Habermas, however, she was not concerned to establish the cognitive grounding of truth claims *at all*, through rational discourse or any other means. She was concerned with the problem of moral judgment, though; and she asserted that human beings can, and ought to, make judgments about the world they live in even though they do not have access to any absolute cognitive standards from which they can derive certainty. Her point is that if we had to rely upon Habermas's ideal communicative conditions (or upon any ideal condition, for that matter) in order to make rational judgments, then we are really admitting that we cannot make judgments with any conviction until such time as we can be certain of the cognitive validity of truth. Judgment – that is, good judgment – is suspended until unconstrained communication is achieved in the world. Arendt was doubtful that such conditions would ever be achieved. She did not exclude the possibility that 'good judgment' might be reflected in the intersubjective consensus of the community, but she rejected Habermas's contention that this consensus is the *necessary* condition for judgment and his assertion that this rational consensus has cognitive truth. In the absence of ideal conditions for intersubjectivity, indeed in the absence of any cognitive basis for validating truth claims, we still have to make judgments, and this presupposes that, as individuals, we must be able in some way to maintain a theoretical detachment from the world of action under any conditions. In sum, whereas Habermas strives for a unity of theory and practice in his ideal communicative discourse, Arendt ultimately defends the necessary separation between theory and practice, and concomitantly the separation between the individual as 'thinker' and the individual as a participant in community.

The necessity for maintaining a separation between thought and action is perhaps made clearer by Stanley Rosen in an article he wrote on 'Thought and Action.'[15] Here Rosen set out to clarify the meaning of these two concepts, beginning with the question: If action is the criterion of thought, how can we formulate the relationship between the two? This was Arendt's starting-point as well. Either action and thought are the same, or they are different, and if they are different, we must be able to make the difference intelligible.

If we start with the proposition, says Rosen, that action is made intelligible by thought, we can draw two different possible conclusions: either thought furnishes the value of action, or the intelligibility of action by thought is separate from the intrinsic value of action. This second possible conclusion is the one that Arendt held as the central thesis of *The Human Condition*. Regardless of the fact that the tradition of political thought consistently interpreted action according to the theoretical model of truth, Arendt insisted that action had an inherent and distinct value that could not be subsumed under theoretical understanding. Rosen takes this proposition – that the value of action is something separate from its intelligibility – and subjects it to two further possible hypothetical queries. (1) If action is intelligible but its intelligibility remains distinct from its true worth, there can be no criteria for intelligibility that have priority. Any coherent system of thought is as good as any other, since none can account for the value of action as a criterion. In other words, theory becomes indiscriminate and itself 'theoretically unintelligible.' This position cannot be reasonably maintained. (2) If action *is* intelligible as the criterion of meaning, then we can assume that the 'value' of action is inherently connected to its ability to be made intelligible. In other words, there is no escaping the fact that action and theory are interrelated. The nature of the problem changes. Now we are confronted with a third element: the thing that unites theory and practice. For Rosen, we cannot speak of the relationship between theory and action without invoking this third component that unites the two. What is it that compels us to assess theoretically the value of action?

These are the very same questions that Arendt raised in her final work, albeit in a much less pointed fashion. There is a tendency in her early work, particularly in *The Human Condition*, to regard all theoretical explanation from Plato to Marx as equal, that is, as equally incapable of expressing the true meaning of action. In the work of 1958 she did seem to think that the intelligibility of action was separate from its real worth. But we find that in her later work she abandoned this 'resentment' towards theory and assumed the contrary position – that action without intelligibility is meaningless. I believe that *The Life of the Mind* represents an attempt to answer Rosen's final question: What is it that compels us to assess theoretically the value of action? The book is an effort to describe the ground that furnishes the connection between theory and action while still maintaining the distinction between them. Rosen maintained that this ground is itself unintelligible, even though we must presume its priority to make any sense at all of theory or action. Arendt did not rest content with this conclusion. She felt that the attempt had to be made to make the unity intelligible in order to salvage both action and thought.

The exploration of *The Life of the Mind* is indeed a conversion from Arendt's early glorification of action, but it is not a conversion to the unworldly rationality of metaphysics or what Habermas called 'an antiquated concept of theoretical knowledge.' It is rather an acknowledgment that the value of action cannot be separated from its intelligibility, nor can action be properly understood as prior to intelligibility. But this is not to say that theory is prior to action, or to suggest that one could grasp the intelligibility of things apart from the *action* that gives the human world substance. Arendt once said: 'I really believe that you can only act in concert and I really believe that you can only think by yourself.'[16] Though they are distinct activities, requiring different conditions for their fulfilment, they are none the less united in the being of the unitary individual. Ultimately, it is the same person who thinks and acts. In laying emphasis upon the ground that brings the thinking 'being' and the acting 'being' together, I think Arendt would have wholeheartedly agreed with Socrates' endeavour. Stanley Rosen expresses the latter well: 'According to Socrates, the city is an image of the soul writ large. We find in the different functions exercised within the city, a magnified and articulated representation of the functions of the soul. The soul is itself incomplete in two senses: its practical possibilities can be achieved only within society, and it is only within society that the possibility of philosophy arises.'[17] From this perspective, we understand that the very possibility for thinking 'by myself' arises only because the city exists to sustain the community of all.

Arendt's emphasis upon thinking in the last part of her life was not, then, a renunciation of action, speech, and plurality, but it was a move away from the notion that these characteristics of the realm of action determine thought. The analysis in *The Life of the Mind* is more complex and more subtle than anything else Arendt wrote for the very reason that she refused to order priorities between action and thought, or between different kinds of thinking. In sum, the shift from action to thinking does make sense.

Thought and Natality

Our second matter for consideration is the following: Does *The Life of the Mind* illuminate for us the 'ground' in which man as actor – in time, in the plural – and man as thinker – solitary and 'timeless' – are united? The work is an elaborate construction of the three-part structure of mental life: thinking, willing, and judging. Arendt intended these three aspects of the mind to cover the whole range of human experience: man as an abstract thinker, as an actor, and as a reflector upon the past. Thinking, willing, and judging are the three activities of the mind through which we make these diverse aspects of our experience intelligible and meaningful. Arendt constantly reminded us that we ought not to 'think' these three activities in isolation from one another, for to do so means that we are violating some fundamental aspect of experience. Concentrating solely upon the timeless experience of thinking, for example, may lead us to believe that we have an essence that is truly outside of time and may induce the hubris that we are inviolable, or autonomous, or that we have access to some realm of eternal truth. Emphasizing the will to the exclusion of the other faculties has even graver consequences. We are in danger of believing that we are free to will the future in any way we want, without any qualifications or restrictions upon our actions. And asserting the primacy of judgment would make us think that the past has some determinant, causal effect upon our capacity to affect the future. All three excesses have become familiar to us, either through the tradition of political thought or in the actions of immoderate people. The over-emphasis upon thinking as man's highest activity has been perhaps the greatest legacy of Western thought, beginning with Plato and culminating in Heidegger's theory of 'being.' The excesses of judging have had an equally powerful, though more modern, impact in the philosophies of history generated by Hegel and Marx and in Nietzsche's doctrine of eternal recurrence. Most threatening of all has been the ascendancy of the will that finds its expression not in philosophy but in the actual attempts by totalitarian states and, in some cases, by science in general to mould the world in an unreflective manner.

In conceiving of the process of mental life as a triumvirate of separate but interrelated loyalties, Arendt thought it possible to understand human activity, to give it a moral content, and at the same time to allow it to be formative. Her depiction of the life of the mind as an activity that is bound by the past and future – the limiting conditions of finite, human existence – and whose very containment by these limiting conditions allows for some impartial, critical questioning, is perhaps too imprecise an image to convey what she really meant. It is difficult to assess this image of Arendt's without imparting a special significance to 'thinking,' especially since she herself assigned thinking a position of first among equals in the tripartite structure of the mind. This 'primacy' is, I believe, what has prompted some commentators to claim that the eternal, or timeless, dimension of the life of the mind was most important to Arendt. Her friend Glenn Gray, who certainly knew her thoughts well, remarked after Arendt's death: 'It is clear that the meaning which the invisible winds of thought make manifest to us extends well beyond the sphere of the human; ... how we can learn to belong to the spheres beyond the human is a theme Hannah Arendt did not live to develop.'[18]

However, Gray 'risk[s] in conclusion a personal observation about the thought Hannah Arendt.'[19] He thinks that Arendt was moving in a direction close to that of Socrates and his connection between thinking and the love of the good. Though Arendt had a tremendous admiration for Socrates, the idea that thinking is grounded in a love of the eternal good is one she rejected throughout her life, and she reiterated this rejection explicitly in *The Life of the Mind*. She insisted that thinking had to be situated in a temporal, human context. For her, the experience of thinking is a 'timeless' one, but the object towards which thought moves is not timeless, but temporal. The image of thought being contained between past and future was a way of conveying this world-bound understanding of thinking. It is clearer perhaps in the following statement made in the context of an assessment of Karl Jaspers: 'The realm [thought] in which Jaspers is at home ... does not lie in the beyond and is not utopian; it is not of yesterday nor of tomorrow; it is of the present and of this world. Reason has created it and freedom reigns in it. It is not something to locate and organize; it reaches into all the conuntries of the globe and into all their pasts. And although it is worldly, it is invisible.'[20] Arendt did not think that the eternal dimension was the anchor of thinking; though we may experience thinking in this way, we must be careful always to relate that experience back to the world. Glenn Gray, then, is imputing a tendency to Arendt's later thought that is simply not there.

Is it conceivable, though, to think about 'thinking' and its consequences for judgment and action without attributing the object of thought to something outside the flux of time? Can we, in following Arendt, imagine that human activity is responsible, just, and moral without satisfying the need to give these things a permanent, substantive content? I think so. Not only *can* we do this, but is is imperative that we do it in order to preserve the idea of responsibility. Yet another peer of Hannah Arendt's, Hans Jonas, has written extensively on the relationship between philosophy, politics, and responsibility in the twentieth century and he gives a compelling account of the worldly ground of thinking.

That thinking must be responsible to the world, even while fleeing it temporarily in order to gain a critical distance, is a position that Jonas shares with Arendt. Jonas rejects the notion that thinking is a form of eros for the same reasons as Arendt: 'The Platonic *eros*, directed at eternity, at the non-temporal, is not responsible for its object. For this "is" and never "becomes." What time cannot affect and to which nothing can happen is an object not of responsibility but of emulation.'[21] The implication of any philosophy that posits an eternal object for thinking, according to Jonas, is that such an object, and the good that accrues from it, is accessible to the individual independent of, and even in abdication of, his responsibilities to the world. Such a conception separates the thinker radically from his being as a creature of time.

Yet the idea of responsibility to the world does demand some concept, some standard, that is to be upheld. What standard can be furnished by temporality, the realm in which values and traditions are constantly changing, and in which human beings are always transforming themselves? To find such a standard, says Jonas, is first of all to acknowledge a concern for 'temporality in its ever-new, always unprecedented productions, which no knowledge of essence can predict.'[22] We have to start, not by admonishing the unpredictability of human affairs, but by celebrating them. We need, in Jonas's words, an 'ontic paradigm' that reaffirms our temporality and yet can furnish an imperative that can guide responsible action. Such a paradigm, he asserts, is found in the fact of natality: 'When asked for a single instance (one is enough to break the ontological dogma) where the coincidence of "is" and "ought" occurs, we can point at the most familiar sight: the newborn, whose mere breathing uncontradictably addresses an ought to the world around, namely, to take care of him. Look and you know.'[23]

The fact of natality places the burden upon us to ensure the continuity of the species, to guarantee that the new human being will be able to act into the future, and to not obstruct the possibilities for his creative potential. This is the responsibility to which Jonas refers. Perhaps most significant of all is that in the newborn's sheer appearance in the world, there lies the capacity for thought, the 'miracle,' as Arendt described it, 'that saves the world.'[24] When Arendt spoke of natality, she usually referred to it as the ontological root of action. Natality – new human beings appearing again and again – interrupts the continuum of history. These unique births are the living testament to freedom. She did not, as far as I know, ever refer explicitly to natality as the limiting condition upon freedom. She did not follow Jonas in referring to natality as the object of thought or responsibility. But she did say something close to it, again in the context of her observations on Karl Jaspers. In praising Jaspers's sanity of thought in the midst of political madness, Arendt marvelled that he was able to sustain this good judgment solely in the weight of his person;[25] even though his reason may have been silent, and therefore politically ineffectual in the short term, it testified to the inherent capacity of the human being to think. The reason that Jaspers exemplified, Arendt said, could be annihilated only if 'all reasonable men are actually, literally slaughtered.'[26] We can draw the meaning of Jonas's remarks about natality and responsibility from this: that our first obligation, in defence of reason, is to preserve and care for the perpetuity of the species, not for the sake of history, but for the promise that every single human being holds in his capacity to think and to act.

Our actions have to be guided by the first general principle: the reverence for life. This first principle would seem to contain within it the moderation that Arendt regarded as crucial to the preservation of the human condition. In revering the 'miracle of birth,' we can accomplish the threefold imperative of the life of the mind. We ensure a commitment to the continuity of the species, and thereby to history. We have an obligation to provide a future for the newborn in which he can act freely. And by dwelling upon the idea of natality, we are reminded of the infinitude of novelty in which thought manifests itself eternally in the phenomena. The miracle of birth is, finally, the ground from which the unity of thought and action stems. Its miraculous nature, though itself perhaps unintelligible, is not without meaning. As Jonas reminds us, the continuous regeneration of the miracle commands our responsibility.

The appeal to natality as the ground of the unity of action and thought may appear to be a vague commitment. It may seem to be turning the obvious into an object of theoretical speculation. But Arendt's special talent lay in illuminating the obvious for us. When we look at her most powerful commentaries on modern society and politics, we can see that natality, or the neglect of it, is at the base of all her concerns. The most ominous characteristic of the totalitarian state, she warned, is that it seeks to make human beings superfluous: 'Terror ... as the obedient servant of natural or historical movement has to eliminate from the process not only freedom in any specific sense, but the very source of freedom which is given with the fact of the birth of man and resides in his capacity to make a new beginning.'[27] Similarly, in her critique of modern science, Arendt wrote: 'Man, insofar as he is a scientist, does not care about his own stature in the universe or about his position on the evolutionary ladder of animal life; this "carelessness" is his pride and his glory. The simple fact that physicists split the atom without any hesitations the very moment they knew how to do it, although they realized full well the enormous destructive potentialities of their operation, demonstrates that the scientist *qua* scientist does not even care about the survivial of the human race on earth or, for that matter, about the survival of the planet itself.'[28]

Arendt's scathing attack on the modern glorification of labour in *The Human Condition* also grew from her fear that natality was being forgotten in modern society. Labour, she argued, is the activity that sustains life, but it sustains life in its perpetual, undifferentiated sense. Labour is the guarantee that the appearance of new human beings is possible, but it does not dwell upon the 'miracle' of the individual appearance. Its concern is continuity. The greatest threat of the labour theories of value is that they exalt the process character of life to the point where the process dwarfs the importance of the uniqueness of each life. The emphasis upon species-life, and labour as its principle, pays the heavy price of diminishing the stature of the individual. The consequences, Arendt remarked in a particularly pessimistic tone, are devastating for modern man. 'The last stage of the laboring society, the society of jobholders, demands of its members a sheer automatic functioning, as though individual life had actually been submerged in the over-all life process of the species and the only active decision still required of the individual were to let go, so to speak, to abandon his individuality ... It is quite conceivable that the modern age – which began with such an unprecedented and promising outburst of human activity – may end in the deadliest, most sterile passivity history has ever known.'[29]

Totalitarian regimes, whose most serious abridgment of the human condition lay in their genocidal plans and in their adherence to ideologies that make human beings 'superfluous,' are then but the most grave manifestations of a tendency in modern society to supersede the limiting conditions of natality. Less grave, but still threatening, efforts to do the same are apparent in the consuming, labouring ethos of Western democracies and in the scientific attitude that anything is possible. Beginning from a commitment to natality – its capacity for newness as well as its responsibility for continuity – would seem to be the only prescriptive advice that we can glean from Arendt's writings.

Political Consequences

We now arrive at our final consideration: What are the political ramifications of such a commitment? There are no indications in *The Life of the Mind* as to what Arendt might have thought about the recovery of political life in the twentieth century. Even in her earlier work she had been cautious about prophesying, or setting out strategies for reform. Surveying her work as a whole, we find that she is generally pessimistic, commenting for example in *The Human Condition* that the modern age may usher in 'the most sterile passivity history has ever known,' and in her reflections on revolutions that the possibility of forming a new concept of the state is 'very slight.' Moreover, she did not endorse a universal attitude towards political action; that is, she did not encourage any sort of binding obligation on individuals to engage in political reform. Her judgments were always reserved for individuals. She condemned Eichmann for not acting because he was in a situation that demanded action. By contrast, she praised Karl Jaspers for his strength in solitude and silence in the midst of political corruption. She never suggested that Jaspers ought to have 'done something' other than what he was best at doing – thinking. She lavished admiration on Rosa Luxemburg for her passionate engagement in 'the destinies of the world,' but Arendt felt no compulsion to dedicate her own life to these same destinies.

In her refusal to impose universal prescriptions for political action, Arendt is at variance with most contemporary theorists of obligation. She would have been uncomfortable, I imagine, in the company of neo-Marxist revolutionaries who call out for programmatic action, and in the company of liberal moral philosophers who want to discover the universal basis of moral obligation. One of the latter, Hannah Pitkin, commented: 'For a political theorist of her stature and range, Hannah Arendt had remarkably little to say about justice.'[30]

Pitkin emphasized in her critique of Arendt that thinking about politics always has to take account of substantive content. Politics engages not simply individuals, but large groups of people who use their collective power to shape a public realm. Surely, Pitkin argued, this means that we are under some specific obligation to ensure that this power is not abused, to ensure that justice is somehow distributed equitably. From Pitkin's perspective, we have an obligation to social justice and this obligation can be fulfilled only in the transition from a private to a public responsibility. This transition takes two forms, she tells us: either we come to politics out of self-interest, drawn to it by need, fear, ambition, or interest, and are subsequently transformed because 'we are forced to find or create a common language of purposes and aspirations' and in the process 'we learn to think about the standards ... of justice, of our community';[31] or we may come to politics out of the intense suffering of deprivation, as for example happens in a revolutionary movement where the oppressed suddenly recognize that theirs is a collectively shared burden. The transition from the private realm – the realm of egoistic self-interest and intensely personal experience (great pain or suffering) – to the public realm, for Pitkin, somehow accomplishes a qualitative transformation in human beings. She writes: 'In the process we learn that we are different than we had thought.'[32] Political commitment and action, for Pitkin, is absolutely necessary for us to actualize our full potential as human beings, *and* for us to grasp the nature of justice.

Pitkin's discussion of the private and public distinctions sounds a hollow echo of Hannah Arendt's *The Human Condition*. What is the 'miracle' of political participation that effects a fundamental transformation in human understanding?

Arendt came to realize half-way through her career that one cannot hang justice on the quality of political engagement. Doing so does not give a greater weight to matters of justice; it actually subjects justice to the sway of public opinions and passions. One need not enter into political action to recognize the importance of justice in human relations. Indeed, one will never know the meaning of justice if one attempts to arrive at it by way of self-interest or through the experience of poverty and acute deprivation.

I do not think that Hannah Pitkin's accusation that Arendt did not consider justice is a fair one. Justice is at the very core of all Arendt's considerations, but she is much closer in spirit to Socrates than to any modern contract theorist or utilitarian. Justice is ultimately a matter of the individual, but the individual lives ∽mongst other men. The individual's obligations are both to himself and to his society. How these obligations will be met, and to what extent one is emphasized over the other, depends entirely upon the context into which one is thrust. The balance between the meaning that commands loyalty from the individual and the meaning that emerges from the free association of public-minded individuals is always a precarious one. The one is never transformed into the other, nor ought the one to be supplanted by the other. Her defence of the individual over and above the society is not a defence in principle, but one that she felt had to be made at this particular juncture in history where the opportunities for political action are constricted. She once said in a public address that in dark times 'much more reliable will be the doubters and skeptics, not because skepticism is good or doubting wholesome, but because [such people] are used to [examining things and making up their own minds]. Best of all will be those who know that whatever else happens, as long as we live we are condemned to live together with ourselves.'[33]

There is something disturbingly apolitical in Arendt's claim that the most reliable people are those who think and act from a concern that as long as they live they are condemned to live with themselves. In this formulation, the basis of justice lies in the urgency of maintaining internal harmony. Not only may the urgency of this desire preclude the possibility of political participation under many circumstances in a democratic polity, but as Arendt herself had pointed out at various points in her career, the inner life is a shadowy, opaque place. 'Seen from the world of appearances, from the marketplace, the thinking ego always lives in hiding, *lathé biōsas*.'[34] Human beings appear to others as unitary selves, whether their inner life is peaceful or not. In the public realm, in which all people appear as indivisible units, there can be no assessment of who is 'best,' that is, most just or virtuous. Human beings are quite capable of appearing as something they are not. The criminal, if his crimes go undetected and unpunished, suffers no consequences for his lack of internal harmony. We cannot help but be reminded here of the oldest challenge to the view that it is better to be just than to be unjust:

Thrasymachus in Book I of the *Republic* counters Socrates by saying that surely it is better to be unjust if one can successfully avoid penalty. Surely it is better to seek one's own advantage.

It is doubtful that Socrates manages to convince Thrasymachus that it is in his own interest to practice justice. In the terms that Thrasymachus and those like him understand advantage – wealth, strength, glory – Socrates' injunction is unpersuasive. Arendt, in claiming that the impetus for thinking is the desire to be in harmony with oneself, has confronted the oldest problem in political philosophy. Why is Arendt's, and Socrates', understanding of the basis of justice unconvincing to many? Why is it not immediately obvious that it is better to suffer injustice than to commit it? Especially since, as Socrates and Arendt agree, this axiom emerges from a concern for oneself. It does not require that one barter away one's own happiness for the sake of an altruistic concern for others. This is Thrasymachus's understanding of justice, and because he sees self-concern only in terms of a greater share of worldly goods, he understandably regards giving up one's acquired goods as unreasonable. What Thrasymachus would have to see, in order to accept Socrates' and Arendt's equation of justice and happiness, is that his deeds and desires may come back to haunt him, and that his unjust acts may cause him a pain that he cannot anticipate. Thrasymachus must be prompted to think, or as Arendt put it in another way, he must be taught to fear his own conscience. What causes a person to fear conscience is not the threat of punishment (particularly if his acts are not perceived as criminal by others), but the 'anticipation of the presence of a witness who awaits him only *if* and when he goes home.'[35]

The fear of conscience, the need to think, is not as universal or as urgent as Arendt would hope. Because people are free to choose among a plurality of ends, there is no guarantee that most people will put internal harmony high on their list of 'goods.' Citing Shakespeare's Richard III, Arendt said that Shakespeare's murderer claims that 'every man that means to live well endeavours ... to live without [conscience],' and 'success in that comes easy because all he has to do is never start the soundless solitary dialogue we call "thinking," never go home and examine things.'[36] The quality and characteristics of the public realm do much to shape how individuals will make choices, as Arendt knew well. The widespread endorsement of the pursuit of wealth, the pursuit of public recognition, and the peculiarly modern pursuit of ideological utopia all militate against the individual's quest for justice, understood as seeking internal harmony. What makes thinking perhaps more difficult in the contemporary world, and at the same time more imperative, is the deficiency of political and institutional supports for it. Here of course we mean thinking as the encouragement of the soundless dialogue with oneself, and not thinking as instrumental or scientific reasoning. Ours is an age in which questions of ultimate meaning are relegated to the silence of private deliberation. One thinks of many serious moral issues at stake: abortion, eugenics research, euthanasia, surrogate motherhood. Society has moved progressively towards regarding these issues as a matter of private concern. In many cases, acts that were considered criminal are no longer regarded as such. Acts that would have solicited threats of eternal damnation no longer command reference to punishment in the afterlife. In a world without public judgment of many actions with moral consequences, and without the fear of hell, the individual is thrown back on himself. We have a particularly hard burden to bear: we must be our own judges, our own condemners, and our own forgivers. We cannot afford *not* to think.

A classic response to the understanding of justice as a kind of thinking comes from Aristotle. Unlike Thrasymachus, who at least agrees with Socrates on one point, that matters of justice and injustice concern individual happiness, Aristotle says that 'justice and injustice always imply more than one person.' One cannot commit injustice against oneself, except in a 'metaphorical and analogical sense.' In the discourses on the question (by which Aristotle means Plato's *Republic* and the writings of his followers), 'a distinction is set up between the rational and irrational parts of the soul; and this is what leads people to suppose that there is such a thing as injustice towards oneself.'[37] Justice may indeed imply more than one person, as Aristotle asserts, but what of acts of injustice that go unacknowledged? What if societies, mores, and laws are in a state of transition or upheaval, so that individuals possibly are not aware that they are committing unjust acts or bearing the consequences of unjust acts? What if, even worse, the victims of injustice are silenced by death, imprisonment, and terror? Injustice may always require a victim, but in a world where the aggrieved are silent, the possibility for justice has not fled. Socrates' and Arendt's teaching about the connections between thinking, justice, and the quest for internal harmony is a teaching for such a world.

Yet Arendt would agree with Aristotle when he writes that 'the best [man] is not he who practises virtue in regard to himself but he who practises it towards others; for that is a difficult task.'[38] In practising virtue towards others, we can do so in our daily interactions with our families, friends, and colleagues, but to practise virtue in its fullest sense, one needs the political arena, acting in public with one's peers. Aristotle says that 'Political Justice means justice as between free and (actually or proportionately) equal persons, living a common life for the purpose of satisfying their needs.'[39] Practising virtue in a way that achieves political justice would probably be Arendt's formula for the most complete human happiness, her description of the 'best man.' To the extent that this kind of life is thwarted, we suffer. She would say that since the possibility for political justice as Aristotle has defined it does not exist currently in this society, the possibility for practising virtue towards others is severely limited. We consequently are pushed into an 'abnormal' kind of activity, appropriate for these times. The abnormal activity is a preoccupation with the inner voice, a relentless Socratic questioning. The dialogue with oneself is a perpetual human need, but it becomes more time-consuming and more onerous when the breakdown of tradition is immanent. Searching for justice primarily within oneself is not a desired way of life, but a way of life initiated by circumstance. 'That while I am alive I must be able to live with myself is a consideration that does not come up politically except in "boundary situations."'[40]

One might object that there is no indication in Arendt's work that the life of the mind and the political life can ever be brought together in a peaceful coexistence. It is as though she were saying: should they coincide, it would be a happy day for both politics and philosophy, but to strain to bring them together is to pervert both activities. Is this merely a restatement of the worn-out contest between the philosopher and the city? In one respect, Arendt can be read this way. It is evident that, for her, one can think independently and critically about society and politics. Even if one is fortunate enough to live in a healthy polity, some detachment from the affairs of the city is necessary for thinking.

That this detachment from the affairs of the city, and from the plurality characteristic of the political world, is always a feature of thinking seemed to Arendt indisputable. There are two 'origins' of the experience of thinking recounted by her in *The Life of the Mind*. One, attributed to the Greeks, is thinking as admiring wonder, and in this account the 'starting point of thinking is neither puzzlement nor surprise nor perplexity' but an experience of 'admiration, confirmation and affirmation.'[41] A second, quite different experience Arendt identifies with the Roman tradition, culminating in Hegel, and in this formulation she says thinking 'arises out of the disintegration of reality and the resulting *dis*unity of man and world, from which springs the need for another world, more harmonious and more meaningful.'[42] What the two 'needs' for thinking have in common, for Arendt, is that 'in both cases, thinking leaves the world of appearances.'[43]

While Arendt emphasized the commonality of the two origins of the experience of thinking – both require a withdrawal from the world – the difference is none the less marked. If we understand the need to think in the way that Arendt attributed to the Greeks, then thinking is an ever-present human need, obviously affected by events in the world, but neither started nor stopped by them. In contrast, thinking as it is depicted by Arendt for the Romans and for Hegel is an activity brought to life by the particular conditions of the world, specifically by bad conditions. We know that Arendt's exemplary thinker is Socrates, not Cicero or Hegel, and this tells us a lot about how she understood the 'origin' of thinking. Though Arendt conceived of thinking as an inner dialogue, not a quietistic reverence, the Greek experience of thinking indicated that even in an integrated reality, the need to think is present, and experienced as a kind of withdrawal. The inner life, though so important for moral considerations, could not, for Arendt, be completely compatible under any conditions with one's life as a member of political community. The dialogue with myself can be recreated under exceptional circumstances with close friends, but it can never mesh with a 'public' self. Efforts to replicate, in the political arena, the internal harmony that I may struggle for in thinking are doomed to failure, disappointment, and possibly tyranny. Arendt ade it clear that the distance between private imperatives and public actions cannot be closed.

> Action in which a We is always engaged in changing our common world, stands in the sharpest possible opposition to the solitary business of thought, which operates in a dialogue between me and myself. Under exceptionally propitious circumstances, that dialogue ... can be extended to another insofar as a friend is as Aristotle said 'another self.' But it can never reach the We, the true plural of action. (An error rather prevalent among modern philosophers who insist upon the importance of communication as a guarantee of truth – chiefly Karl Jaspers and Martin Buber, with his I-thou philosophy – is to believe that the intimacy of the dialogue, the 'inner action' in which I 'appeal' to myself or to the 'other self,' Aristotle's friend, Jaspers' beloved, Buber's THOU, can be extended and become paradigmatic for the political sphere.)[44]

One cannot hope to be everyone's friend, though one needs friends to be able to think. Arendt's blockade on the limits to friendship is similar to Aristotle's. Concord is certainly mandatory for healthy political exchange, and particularly for the sort of mutual respect that Arendt endorsed as the basis for democratic politics, but this is not the same as friendship. Aristotle says in the *Ethics* that 'if men are friends, there is no need of justice between them,' and yet the 'highest form of justice seems to have an element of friendly feeling in it.'[45] What Aristotle seems to mean here in this enigmatic combination of statements is that when one tries to imagine the most complete justice, one imagines the relationship between friends, and the reason that justice between them is complete (hence redundant) is because friends are equal in all things. For Aristotle, equality in friendship means primarily 'equal in quantity'; he goes so far as to say that friends who develop wide differences in virtue, vice, or wealth no longer expect to be friends.[46] But in what Aristotle deems the sphere of justice, that is to say in our dealings with those who are not our equals in all things, hence not our friends, equality means primarily equal proportionate to desert.

If, as Arendt often said, the characteristic feature of the political realm is plurality, then friendship can never become the basis of political relations. To ask that citizens be friends is to ask that all people in one's community be equal, following Aristotle, in wealth and in virtue. Arendt's objections to this model of political life rest not so much on its impracticality as they do on its undesirability. To ask that citizens be equal in wealth and virtue is to consider oneself competent to determine what the standards for equality in such things consist of, and subsequently to ensure that these standards are met. This is a recipe for tyranny and an attitude towards political life that manacles the unpredictability and freedom of human action. The task of human beings 'in the plural' – regardless of the type of regime – is 'changing our common world.' Contrarily, the task of friends is to achieve a harmony, an equilibrium. Citizenship for Arendt is about acting; friendship, whether with oneself or another, is about thinking. We should not be saddened or disturbed by the fact that the configurations of the political world keep changing; in fact, we should rejoice that such dynamism is possible; but we necessarily must be saddened when distances of opinion, wealth, or simply time interrupt the harmony, the equilibrium of friendship.

For Arendt, one needs citizenship and friendship to have a good life. They hold differing promises for happiness and neither is dispensable without cost. She came to value friendship more in her later years, but only because conditions in the world led her to this choice, not because it took the place of active citizenship. It is very important to grasp the following about Arendt: the preoccupation with the inner life, and the close circle of friends, is not a model for human happiness but a prescription for these times in particular. Socrates, Arendt's model of a human being, 'unified two apparently contradictory passions, for thinking and acting.' Arendt admired him because he was a man 'who did not shun the market-place, who was a citizen among citizens,'[47] though she was certainly aware that for refusing to quell his passion for citizenship in the age in which he lived Socrates 'lay down his life.'[48] We would not expect such sacrifice from ordinary human beings, which is why Socrates remains mythical in his heroism, and why we forgive those who forgo active citizenship for friendship in dark times, and do not judge them harshly for their recalcitrance.

Where Arendt would assuredly depart from the account that some thinkers give of the life of the philosopher versus the life of the citizen is in her contention that the solitary life of the philosopher is not preferable to the life of the actor. It is preferable only in extreme cases where bad political conditions make withdrawal and solitude a necessary course of action. The life of the mind needs the political world, though, as its natural habitat: it can never escape that fact. Even in the worst of political situations, the attachment to the city and to the world of plurality has to be recollected as the proper ground of theorizing. From this standpoint, a life of withdrawal is never a preferred choice, but a necessary one forced upon the individual by circumstances. Arendt's understanding of the worldly ground of thought is best expressed in the following comments from her essay on Lessing and humanity in dark times: 'Flight from the world in dark times of impotence can always be justified as long as reality is not ignored, but is constantly acknowledged as the thing that must be escaped. When people choose this alternative, private life too can retain a by no means insignificant reality, even though it remains impotent. Only it is essential for them to realize that the realness of this reality consists not in its deeply personal note, any more than it springs from privacy as such, but inheres in the world from which they have escaped.'[49]

The demarcation between the life of the mind and the life of action becomes a sharp, obvious one only at those critical times when the two are separated into distinct ways of life. The alienation of the philosopher from the city, for Arendt, is always an aberration, a temporary mode of existence and not an alienation that is fundamental to the activity of the philosopher. As Barry Clarke noted, even in his radical separation from the world the 'thinker' bears within his activity the possibility for politics. The 'true freedom' of the mind that 'makes its appearance only when values fundamental to the human condition are at stake' manifests itself initially as critical, private distance, but this resistance can become 'political and communal when an indiidual takes his place in the alternative community.'[50] The alternative community may lead to new political formations, as for example Arendt claimed was the case in the French Resistance; those who participated in the movement 'had been visited for the first time in their lives by an apparition of freedom.'[51] Sometimes, however, the number of resisters is too small, or the political 'space' too tightly controlled, for any alternative community to emerge. Even in these cases, the withdrawal of thought is not wasted, nor is it ineffectual. For these thoughts still belong to the world and will perhaps be remembered by subsequent generations who will draw courage and inspiration from them. Sometimes, all that remains is the 'uncertain, flickering and often weak light that some men and women, in their lives and their works, will kindle under almost all circumstances.'[52]

For Arendt, the degree to which thinking against the current produces an alternative community, a new kind of action, is contingent. The potential for reform through resistance is important, but it is not the reason for resisting. Hence, she did not judge the worth of the Resistance fighters to be in any way superior to the integrity of the lone resister in Nazi Germany. She would simply have said that to judge a man's actions, you have to look at the particular situation in which he found himself. Power, as she said, referring to the exemplary case of the American Revolution, can grow up only where there are numbers of people who 'get together and bind themselves through promises, covenants and mutual pledges.'[53] This power remained for Arendt mysterious in its origin. It is something that exists prior to the act of contracting and pledging; it is not, as Hannah Pitkin suggested, created by it. Covenants and pledges are in themselves useless if they are built upon erroneous conceptions of the ends of life, or if they are entered into by human beings who do not comprehend the importance of freedom.

Arendt has been criticized as much for what she did not address as she has been for her own words. In particular, she has been castigated for her neglect of questions of justice. Yet her work testifies to a consuming concern with justice, if we understand by that a preoccupation with thinking, moral responsibility, and internal harmony. As has been demonstrated, the 'Socratic turn' lies at the heart of Arendt's political philosophy. When her critics chastise her for neglecting justice, they mean more precisely distributive justice, and it is certainly true that Arendt did not give much attention to matters of this sort. Recalling Aristotle's distinction between justice in friendship and justice in the political realm, we note that justice in friendship requires an equality of peers in all things whereas justice in political matters requires an equality proportionate to desert. Assessing equality proportionate to desert requires prudence, and a sensitivity to particular circumstances, cultures, and history. We know this well from Aristotle. In differing regimes, differing things are valued and consequently varying claims will be made upon distributive justice. Societies develop their own particular understandings of what constitutes a 'just' distribution of equal and unequal shares, based upon widely differing criteria: military honour, education, scientific achievement, entrepreneurship, just to name a few. Arendt was always impressed by the 'manifoldness' of political communities, by their varieties of form, and by their ultimately mysterious origins. She departed from Aristotle only in thinking that the possibility for variation was much more extensive than he (or Montesquieu, another great classifier of regimes) could have imagined.

> The manifoldness of ... communities is evinced in a great many different forms and shapes, each obeying different laws, having different habits and customs, and cherishing different memories of the past, i.e., a manifoldness of traditions. Montesquieu was probably right in assuming that each such entity moved and acted according to a different inspiring principle, recognized as the ultimate standard for judging the community's deeds and misdeeds – virtue in republics, honor and glory in monarchies, moderation in aristocracies, fear and suspicion in tyrannies – except that this enumeration, guided by the oldest distinction between forms of government (as the rule of one, of a few, of the best, or of all) is of course pitifully inadequate to the rich diversity of human beings living together on the earth.[54]

Just as the forms of community are richly diverse, so too are the kinds of domination and exploitation that can take place within them. It is an old lesson of politics that those who are unequal in some things (such as money) tend to think themselves unequal, that is, better, in all things, including virtue. Likewise, those who are equal in some things, such as freedom, tend to think themselves equal in all things, including virtue. It is in the nature of political communities, composed of a plurality of individuals and groups, that there will be some mixture of equalities and inequalities, and that individuals and groups will confuse, manipulate, and seek to change the balance between them. This is not to trivialize the importance of questions of distributive justice: assessing what the balance of interests and powers is in any given political community is an important task for political thinkers. But it is not the only one, and for Arendt it was not the most crucial one. One cannot begin to analyse the 'rules' for distribution unless one has a reflective understanding of ends, and Arendt's principal concern was that we are making up rules all the time without pausing to think. Arendt saw her responsibility as a political thinker in thinking about freedom and justice. She sought to comprehend what these things mean and how they could be framed in ways intelligible to people living in the rubble of a spent philosophical tradition. It is not an unfitting parallel to say that she is a Socrates, not an Aristotle, for the twentieth century.

Arendt did not ever speak of the problem of the distribution of wealth in an advanced capitalist society, or of property relations in general, or of the status of women, or any of the other issues that dominate political discourse in our time. We do know, though, that she felt that far too much attention was being focused upon the 'economic base' of modern society. She wrote in *The Human Condition* that ours is 'a society of labourers which is about to be liberated from the fetters of labor, and this society does no longer know of those other higher and more meaningful activities for the sake of which this freedom would deserve to be won.'[55]

Arendt's criticism of labour and of the reduction of all life to the labouring mentality in *The Human Condition* was not intended to be a call to halt social planning, or to give up the effort to improve the material conditions for the poor and disadvantaged. In fact, she thought that the improvement of life for all members of society and the redistribution of wealth was so obvious a goal that it did not warrant serious debate.[56] She must have realized that such propositions are in fact submitted to endless debate, that most debates in politics evolve precisely around the distribution of goods. But Arendt's fear was that as long as political concerns are polarized between those who feel that protecting private property is the sole aim of politics, and those who feel that emancipation from private property will lead automatically to an improved political life, we are not grasping the real problem. She remarked, rather offhandedly: 'You know, somehow, Marx still believed that if you leave men alone – society corrupts man – and change society, man will reappear. He will reappear – God protect us from it: this optimism runs throughout history.'[57]

Arendt's objective was to draw our attention away from the social issues, not because they are unimportant, but because if we invest all our energies in social emancipation, we lose sight of the goals of this emancipation. If we do not have any coherent sense of what freedom is in its best possible manifestation, if we simply put the issue off until such time as we think we have achieved the necessary conditions for its attainment, we will never know if the conditions have been met since we have no idea of what we are aiming for. This is why the society of labourers and consumers threatens to become a permanent process, 'dazzled by the abundance of its growing fertility.'[58]

Arendt's reflections on the labouring society remained unchanged. At least she never raised the subject again in any depth after she wrote *The Human Condition*. What few comments she made in passing do not contradict what she wrote there. If anything, she became more intent upon deflecting attention away from the social concerns towards an inquiry into the ontological foundation of freedom. In spite of the reputation with which she has been saddled by some camps – that of a great systematizer – she was not a systematic thinker in the tradition of Hegel or Aristotle. Whole aspects of existence, as I have mentioned, are left out of her inquiries. She did not examine the realm of the household (except by inference in her 'Reflections on Litle Rock'); she did not look at the impact of economic relations on political life; and the aesthetic dimension of life is rarely mentioned. The narrow vision with which Arendt pursued her one major concern, the relationship of the individual thinker to the community, may have inhibited her from making some practical suggestions for political regeneration. Yet it is her polemical style and her unwavering concentration that make her such a forceful critic. Her friend Hans Jonas made these remarks about Hannah Arendt at her funeral: 'Things looked different after she looked at them. Thinking was her passion, and thinking with her was a moral activity. She was intensely moral, but completely unmoralistic. Whatever she had to say was important, often provoca-tive, sometimes wrong, but never trivial, never negligible, never to be forgotten again. Even her errors were more worthwhile than the verities of many lesser minds.'[59]

Arendt devoted her intellectual energy principally to something she felt suffered a diremptive imbalance in the modern world: the place of thought. She sought to restore thinking to some dignity among the process theories of historical materialism, psychological determinism, and even science. Arendt's most important contribution to the history of political theory, I believe, is her example of how one should think. Thought and politics may not always exist in harmony with one another, thought alone will not produce genuine political action, but she taught that of one thing we can be certain: if we do not think, we shall never be able to act freely and responsibly. I can think of no better way to sum up Hannah

Arendt's contribution to political thinking than to repeat the words of Ernest Vollrath: 'Understanding is the promise existing in the world for those who will act in the world after us.'[60] Hannah Arendt has left us this promise.

Notes

Introduction

1 Human plurality is the basic condition of action and speech, Arendt says, and it is through this plurality that the human being reveals itself as distinct and free. She wrote: 'If action as beginning corresponds to the fact of birth, if it is the actualization of the human condition of natality, then speech corresponds to the fact of distinctness and is the actualization of the human condition of plurality, that is, of living as a distinct and unique being among equals' (*The Human Condition*, 178).

2 Ibid., 176

3 The intention to reject a theoretical account of the *vita activa* is reflected in the following statement: 'My use of the term *vita activa* presupposes that the concern underlying all its activities is not the same as and is neither superior nor inferior to the central concern of the *vita contemplativa*' (ibid., 17).

4 The continuity through the tradition of Western thought is identified, according to Arendt, by the juxtaposition of 'Being' to 'Appearances.' This dualism first appears in Plato. In his allegory of the cave, Plato refers to the phenomenal world as a shadowy existence that is less 'real' than the non-appearing realm of essences. By dichotomizing being and appearances, Plato established a dualism between thought and action that has permeated all subsequent political thought. To Arendt, this dualism *in itself* is far more important to consider than its various interpretations. Since Plato, she remarked, 'academic philosophy has ... been dominated by the never-ending reversals of idealism and materialism, of transcendentalism and immanentism, of realism and nominalism, of hedonism and asceticism, and so on' (ibid., 292).

5 Ibid., 17

6 Arendt wrote in her introduction to *The Life of the Mind* that the 'metaphysical fallacies' are actually our *only* indicators of the very real experience of thinking:

'None of the systems, none of the doctrines transmitted to us by the great thinkers may be convincing or even plausible to modern readers; but none of them, I shall try to argue here, is arbitrary, and none can be simply dismissed as sheer nonsense. On the contrary, the metaphysical fallacies contain the only clues we have to what thinking means to those who engage in it – something of great importance today and about which, oddly enough, there exist few direct utterances' (*Life of the Mind*, 1:12).

Chapter 1: In Defence of Action

1 *Human Condition*, 2
2 Ibid., 9–10
3 Ibid., 9
4 Ibid., 20. This passage is critically important for what Arendt had to say much later in her reconsiderations of thought in *The Life of the Mind* (1978). The *nunc stans* of the philosopher is a main topic of that study.
5 Ibid., 14
6 Ibid., 31
7 Ibid., 38
8 Ibid., 31
9 Ibid., 96
10 Ibid., 100
11 Ibid., 120
12 Ibid., 118
13 Ibid., 134
14 Ibid., 144
15 Ibid., 222
16 Ibid., 227
17 Ibid., 229
18 Ibid., note 71
19 'The manifestation of who the speaker and doer unexchangeably is, though it is plainly visible, retains a curious intangibility that confounds all efforts toward unequivocal verbal expression' (ibid., 181).
20 *Human Condition*, 181
21 Ibid., 184
22 Ibid., 185
23 Ibid., 185–6
24 This view is made clear in the following passage: 'The only character of the world by which to gauge its reality is its being common to us all, and common sense occupies such a high rank in the hierarchy of political qualities because it is the one

sense that fits into reality as a whole our five strictly individual senses and the strictly particular data they perceive' (ibid., 208). Arendt referred to common sense throughout her life as a 'sixth sense': the sense that makes us at home in the world. 'There we are and no questions asked' (*Life of the Mind*, 1:59).

25 *Human Condition*, 208
26 Ibid., 211
27 Arendt wrote that the 'faith in *dynamis* (and consequently in politics ... had already come to an end when the first political philosophies were formulated,' although the celebration of the *vita activa* in Greece bestowed upon political activity a certain esteem which has survived in some form throughout the Western tradition (ibid., 205).
28 Ibid., 212
29 Ibid., 153, 154
30 Ibid., 158
31 Ibid.
32 Ibid., 145
33 Ibid., 323
34 With respect to scientific inquiry, Arendt commented that it 'acts into nature from the standpoint of the universe and not into the web of human relationships [and therefore] lacks the revelatory character of action as well as the ability to produce stories and become historical, which together form the very source from which meaningfulness springs into and illuminates human existence' (ibid., 324).
35 Ibid., 167
36 Ibid., 324
37 Ibid., 325
38 Sheldon Wolin expressed something akin to this view in his article 'Hannah Arendt and the Ordinance of Time.' Looking at Arendt's condemnation of the dominace of *animal laborans*, Wolin suggested that the object of Arendt's critique might be misplaced; in fact, we live in a world where 'mind [not labour] is triumphant.' Wolin concluded: 'The encroachments, then, are not those of labour into the political realm. They are instead the encroachments of mind into both realms, the realm of politics and the realm of work. The tyranny of the mind may be the cruelest of tyrannies for it brooks no appeal except to itself' (p. 104).
39 *Human Condition*, 313, footnote
40 Alvarez, 'State of Man,' 337
41 Kenneth Boulding, 'Philosophy, Behavioural Science and the Nature of Man,' 272
42 *Political Thought of Hannah Arendt*, 54
43 Review of *The Human Condition* and Ortega y Gasset's *Man and Crisis* (New York: W.W. Norton and Co. 1958), *Political Science Quarterly* (Summer 1959), 422

44 Bennett, *American Anthropologist*, 684
45 Ibid., 686
46 Canovan, *Political Thought of Hannah Arendt*, 77
47 Ibid., 75
48 That this is true for Arendt is evident in her writings in *On Revolution* (1963). Commenting upon the council movement in the Hungarian revolution of 1956, Arendt held that the councils represented some hope for political action in the twentieth century precisely because, though constituted largely by workers, their objectives were 'primarily political, with social and economic claims playing a very minor role' (p. 274). What is required of political actors, she said, is 'trustworthiness, personal integrity, capacity of judgment and often, physical courage.' None of these qualities is the property of the worker qua *animal laborans*, but rather is a permanent capacity of man insofar as he can transcend the particularity of his function as labourer or worker.
49 Arendt went on in *On Revolution* to give an account of the defeat of the council system in Hungary. According to her, overwhelming pressure from society, political parties, and other 'non-political' variables defeated the efforts of the workers in Hungary. See chapter 6: 'The Revolutionary Tradition and Its Lost Treasure.'
50 Canovan, *Political Thought of Hannah Arendt*, 113, 124
51 Arendt had written in *The Origins of Totalitarianism* that 'the central events of our time are not less effectively forgotten by those committed to a belief in an unavoidable doom, than by those who have given themselves up to reckless optimism' (Preface to the first edition [1973], July 1967).
52 Alvarez, 'State of Man,' 337
53 Found in Melvyn Hill, ed., *Recovery of the Public World*
54 Ibid., 54
55 Ibid., 49–50
56 Ibid., 57
57 We know from *The Human Condition* that Arendt accepted the classical distinction between the private and public realms, but rejected a hierarchical ordering of the *vita activa* and the *vita contemplativa*. It can be argued convincingly that without an understanding of the *vita contemplativa* as man's highest form of activity, the distinction between private and public realms of activity cannot be maintained. This takes some exposition of the classical understanding, however, which I shall undertake at a later stage in the book.
58 Bakan, 'Hannah Arendt's Concepts of Labour and Work,' 58
59 Preface to the first edition of *Origins of Totalitarianism*, viii
60 Ibid., ix
61 'Tradition and the Modern Age,' in *Between Past and Future* (1961), 17

62 Ibid., 17–18
63 Ibid., 24
64 Arendt made a point of saying that in no way can these thinkers be held responsible for the state of affairs in the modern world. Always, she makes the argument that the course of the world is determined by events, not thoughts. However, this does not mean that thoughts are unconnected to events. When Arendt wanted to understand the modern world, she turned to those thinkers who made the most rigorous attempt to interpret it. She always looked to the great philosophers of the past as guide-posts. For Arendt, there is characteristically a 'time lag' between the concerns of the theorist and the manifestation of those same concerns in the general population, although she claimed that one could never prove a causal connection between what the philosopher says and what people do. Perhaps we can put it best by sying that, to Arendt, the 'thinker' takes on the mysterious role of the 'fortune teller' of history.

Commenting on the role of philosophers in history, Arendt said: 'Neither the silence of the tradition nor the reaction of thinkers against it in the nineteenth century can ever explain what actually happened. The non-deliberate character of the break gives it an irrevocability which only events, never thoughts, can have ... On the level of mere thought, which could hardly be concerned then with more than the essentially negative experiences of foreboding, apprehension, and ominous silence, only radicalization, not a new beginning and reconsideration of the past, was possible' ('Tradition and the Modern Age,' 27–8).
65 'The Concept of History,' in *Between Past and Future*, 65
66 Ibid., 79
67 'The fundamental fact about the modern concept of history is that it arose in the same sixteenth and seventeenth centuries which ushered in the gigantic development of the natural sciences. Foremost among the characteristics of that age, which are still alive and present in our own world, is the world-alienation of man ... which is so difficult to perceive as a basic condition of our whole life because out of it, and partly at least out of its despair, did arise the tremendous structure of the human artifice we inhabit today' (ibid., 513).
68 'This process is incapable of guaranteeing man any kind of immortality because its end cancels out and makes unimportant whatever went before: in the classless society the best mankind can do with history is to forget the whole unhappy affair, whose only purpose was to abolish itself' (ibid., 79, 80).
69 Ibid., 54
70 Ibid., 57
71 Ibid., 79
72 'Tradition and the Modern Age,' 40
73 'The Concept of History,' 42
74 Arendt actually spoke of natality as the 'miracle that saves the world, the realm of

human affairs, from its normal "natural" ruin … It is, in other words, the birth of new men and the new beginning, the action they are capable of by virtue of being born' (*Human Condition*, 247).

75 'The Concept of History,' 42

76 This 'tendency,' according to Arendt, constituted the paradox of Greek tragedy.

77 'The Concept of History,' 85

78 Ibid., 47

79 Arendt emphasized that the construing of human life in the image of biological life had different implications for the philosopher and the common man. The latter could assure his 'immortality' by begetting children, hence taking part in what Plato thought to be the natural cycle of nature (but which Arendt thought to be taking part in *human* 'nature,' that is, the chain of human being). The philosopher, however, could participate in eternity in a higher form, through contemplation. What both forms of participation in nature had in common was that they detracted from the capacity man has to immortalize his own unnatural and creative deeds. In the Platonic conception, the only immortality accorded man is his participation in the eternal, natural cycle (ibid., 47).

80 Ibid., 43

81 'Action and "The Pursuit of Happiness"' (1962), 2

82 *Partisan Review* (1946)

83 Arendt said that Kant's 'tranquillity' could be explained by the fact that 'he was strongly rooted in the tradition that philosophy is essentially identical with contemplation – a tradition which Kant himself unconsciously destroyed' (ibid., 42).

84 Ibid., 43

85 Ibid., 46, footnote

86 Ibid., 47

87 Ibid., 50

88 Ibid., 53

89 Ibid., 54

90 Ibid., 56

91 'Understanding and Politics,' 377

92 Ibid., 380

93 Ibid., 391

94 Ibid., 392

95 *Human Condition*, 272

96 Ibid., 272–3

97 Arendt's ambivalence towards philosophy is expressed well by George Kateb. 'I believe that Arendt's deep wish is that thinkers had turned away from their absorption in mind and in metaphysics – if only they could have. But they could not; she knows it. Her deep wish is not her deepest: if men were to "cease to ask

unanswerable questions, [they] would lose not only the ability to produce those thought-things that we call works of art but also the capacity to ask all the unanswerable questions upon which every civilization is founded"' (*Hannah Arendt: Politics, Conscience, Evil*, 194). Kateb makes this judgment about Arendt in the context of his remarks about *Life of the Mind*, yet I think Arendt's 'deep' and 'deepest' wishes, as Kateb describes them, are evident early in her career.

98 *Origins of Totalitarianism*, new edition, 459

99 It is interesting to note that Arendt received criticism from all sides of the philosophical spectrum for her notion that responsible action and thought grows out of the shared opinion of the political world. Two such critics are Jürgen Habermas ('Hannah Arendt's Communications Concept of Power') and Eric Voegelin (review of *The Origins of Totalitarianism*, 1953). While these two thinkers have very different orientations in their political thought, they both held that Arendt's concept of political community was untenable.

Habermas noted that Arendt failed to take account of 'inconspicuously working communications blocks' that can, and do, lead to self-deception on the part of men. Because Arendt wanted to sever political action from all considerations of material concern, she was unable to distinguish between illusory and non-illusory convictions. By locating meaning simply in the expression of opinion, Arendt could not sustain a coherent, critical commentary on what was ailing modern societies. The only criterion by which one can judge political communities, according to her, is the ability of a community to make and keep promises. If that trust is broken, and it often has been, there is no recourse for understanding political power. Thus, Habermas concluded that 'Hannah Arendt finally places more trust in the venerable figure of the contract than in her own concept of a praxis, which is grounded in the rationality of practical judgment. She retreats instead to the contract theory of natural law' (p. 24).

Voegelin took issue with Arendt on much the same point. He said that her thoughts on totalitarianism 'reflect a typically liberal, progressive, pragmatist attitude toward philosophical probems' (p. 75). In locating both the problem and the solution of modernity in the collected 'reason' of political opinion, Arendt confused essences with appearances. Contrary to Habermas, however, who suggested that Arendt ought to have looked more deeply into the possibility of a working praxis, Voegelin adheres to the classical position that knowledge is based on personal insight. For Voegelin, Nature (and hence, human 'nature') is a philosophical concept denoting that which, by definition, cannot be changed. He took exception to Arendt's claim that meaning is found in the collected opinions of plural communities, and to her simultaneous claim that communities can destroy meaning.

In sum, then, both Habermas and Voegelin suggested that Arendt's faith in political action, or opinion, as sufficient ground for understanding legitimate power and meaning, was naïve. Both criticized her for her emphasis on the realm of appearances, and both commented that there is more to be gained in probing what is behind this realm. I think these criticisms are unduly harsh. It is true that Arendt wanted to stay as close to the realm of appearances as possible, and we have already seen why this was so. However, she certainly did not believe in the simple revelatory capacity of phenomena, or politics, and she did try to articulate a critical stance from which to judge the illusory or non-illusory character of action. But this stance comes much later in *The Life of the Mind*, which was published after Habermas's and Voegelin's critiques.

100 p. 324
101 *Life of the Mind*, 1:5

Chapter 2: Acting in the Realm of Appearances

1 *Origins of Totalitarianism*, Preface to the first edition (Summer 1950), vii. In 1966 Arendt wrote a new preface to the book, in which she admitted that the tone of the earlier preface had been overly 'dark.' In this second preface she said that her mood had passed from one of 'speechless outrage and horror' to one of 'grief and sorrow.' None the less, she included the earlier one in the revised edition of the book 'in order to indicate the mood of those years' (ibid., Preface to part 3 [1966], xxiv).

2 Ibid., 461

3 2nd ed., ed. C. Friedrich, 1965; 1st ed., 1956

4 In fact, Friedrich and Arendt aired their differences in a public forum held in 1954. Friedrich remarked that he felt that some authors had wrongly stressed 'peculiar moral obtuseness' as the most important feature of totalitarian states. Arendt replied as follows: '[Mr Friedrich's] remarks may well have been addressed to me and my writings, yet I do not believe I am wrong in finding this is one of those basic distinctions with which we are both concerned. The point ... is ... that "totalitarian indifference" to moral considerations is actually based upon a reversal of all our legal and moral concepts, which ultimately rest on the commandment, "Thou shalt not kill."' Discussion on 'The Nature of Totalitarianism,' part 2 in Carl Friedrich, ed., *Totalitarianism*, Proceedings of a conference held at the American Academy of Arts and Sciences, March 1953, pp. 58, 78.

5 Arendt had a passionate dislike of psychoanalytic theory. She thought that its emphasis on the formative influence of family background and environment served to excuse the individual from his responsibilities as a free, wilful agent. This came out particularly strongly in her reflections on the Eichmann trial, where she said that theories based on such assumptions as the Oedipus complex are an escape from the personal responsibility of those who commit criminal acts (*Eichmann in Jerusalem* [1964], 297).

6 *Origins of Totalitarianism*, 344

7 'What Is Existenz Philosophy?' 50

8 Ibid.

9 *Origins of Totalitarianism*, 438

10 Ibid., 476

11 Buchheim, *Totalitarian Rule*, 14. The best account of classical tyranny is probably to be found in Xenophon's *Hiero or Tyrannicus*, in Leo Strauss, ed., *On Tyranny*. In his commentary, Strauss says that modern tyrannies are distinguished from classical ones by their employment of ideology and technology: 'In contradistinction to classical tyranny, present-day tyranny has as its disposal "technology" as well as "ideologies"' (p. 22). Arendt singled out these same two factors as the essential components of totalitarianism.

12 The phrase 'island of resistance' is borrowed from Carl Friedrich, who singled resistance out as one of the most significant features of totalitarian rule. Though internal resistance is not powerful enough (without external support) to overthrow totalitarian regimes, 'such islands of resistance are ... eloquent testimonials to the strength of human character.' (Friedrich and Brzezinski, *Totalitarian Dictatorship and Autocracy*, 239)

13 Solzhenitsyn, *The Gulag Archipelago* (1978), 3:475

14 Ibid., 2:615

25 *Origins of Totalitarianism*, 470

16 Ibid., 315

17 Ibid., 311

18 Ibid., 478

19 Ibid., 470

20 Ibid., 471

21 Ibid., 475

22 'Hannah Arendt on Hannah Arendt,' in Melvin Hill, ed., *The Recovery of the Public World*, 313–14

23 *Origins of Totalitarianism*, 462

24 Ibid.

25 Arendt thought that this split between the 'extra-temporal' standards of justice and the practical affairs of men had originated with Plato, was assimilated by the Romans, and gained its most powerful sanction in Christian doctrine; but she wrote that it 'seems as though it has only been in the Christian era that Plato's invisible spiritual yardsticks, by which the visible, concrete affairs of men were to be measured and judged, have unfolded their full political effectiveness' ('What Is Authority?' in *Between Past and Future*, 127).

26 Ibid., 121

27 Ibid., 125

28 Ibid., 127
29 Ibid., 127–8
30 *Origins of Totalitarianism*, 462
31 Ibid., 463
32 Ibid., 473
33 Arendt, 'What Is Authority? in *Between Past and Future*, 128
34 Robert C. Tucker held that the Purge Trials in Moscow in 1938, for example, were intended for just such purposes: to terrorize the general population and to eliminate all dissenting opinion. The trials were 'to end all this, to eliminate the Bolshevik habits of criticism and opposition as well as the men who personified these habits, and to create for [Stalin] an autocracy as absolute as any that ever existed' (*The Great Purge Trial*, xxix). Tucker's book is cited frequently in *The Origins of Totalitarianism*.

　　That Arendt considered the use of terror to be the key factor in maintaining a totalitarian state is brought home in her reflections on the 1956 Hungarian Revolution. Part of her explanation for this 'moment' of freedom was that the 'extreme situations of solitary confinement and of torture' were not as prevalent in the satellite states of the USSR as in the central power. Hence in spite of ideological rhetoric and domination there was more space in the absence of terror to generate rebellion ('Totalitarian Imperialism: Reflections on the Hungarian Revolution' [1958], 25).
35 *Origins of Totalitarianism*, 435
36 Ibid., 392
37 *Origins of Totalitarianism*, 457
38 Ibid., 466
39 *Human Condition*, 324
40 *Between Past and Future*, 149
41 Voegelin, 'The Origins of Totalitarianism,' 68–76
42 'A Reply,' 76–84
43 Voegelin, 'The Origins of Totalitarianism,' 75
44 Ibid., 74
45 Ibid., 75
46 'A Reply,' 80
47 Ibid., 84
48 Kateb, 'Arendt and Representative Democracy,' 20–59
49 Wolin, 'Hannah Arendt: Democracy and the Political,' 3–19
50 Ibid., 6, 7
51 'Freedom as a political phenomenon was coeval with the rise of the Greek city-states.' That is, freedom resided in the public space where equal citizens engaged in a peerage of ruling and being ruled' (*On Revolution*, 30).
52 Ibid., 21
53 Arendt was resigned to the fact that violence may be an integral part of new begin-

nings in politics. 'Violence, being instrumental by nature, is rational to the extent that it is effective in reaching the end that must justify it' (*On Violence*, 79). Where violence becomes illegitimate, she claimed, is when it becomes an end in itself. The successful revolution uses violence only as a necessary instrument to achieve power. Power is the end of revolutions and power is defined by Arendt as that which 'springs up whenever people get together and act in concert' (p. 52).

54 *On Revolution*, 35

55 Ibid., 111, 112

56 Ibid., 94

57 'Although the whole record of past revolutions demonstrates beyond doubt that every attempt to solve the social question with political means leads into terror, and that it is terror which sends revolutions to their doom, it can hardly be denied that to avoid this fatal mistake is almost impossible when a revolution breaks out under conditions of mass poverty' (*On Revolution*, 112).

58 Ibid., 68

59 Ibid., 93

60 Robert Nisbet, 'Hannah Arendt and the American Revolution,' 68

61 *On Revolution*, 120

62 Ibid., 131

63 Ibid., 275

64 Ibid., 275, 276

65 Ibid., 277

66 Ibid., 279

67 Ibid., 277

68 Ibid., 276

69 'Totalitarian Imperialism,' 8, 30

70 Ibid., 23

71 Ibid., 32

72 Arendt, 'Rosa Luxemburg: 1871–1919,' in *Men in Dark Times* (1968), 52

73 *On Revolution*, 221. The vehemence with which Arendt maintained the distinction between the political and the social is perhaps best illustrated in a very controversial article she wrote on the subject of bussing and school desegregation in the Southern states. Arendt claimed that this legislation was wrongfully attempting to enforce social equality. She maintained that education was a matter of social, not political concern, and that equality can only be enforced in the legal-political sense. To legislate non-discrimination in social matters was for her not only a confusion of categories but in fact a denial of people's right of association, which Arendt thought was the prerogative of social relations. She wrote: 'The moment social discrimination is abolished, the freedom of society is violated' ('Reflections on Little Rock' [1959], 53).

To Arendt, this 'burning' issue represented one more step towards the annihilation of the political ideal of plurality by attempting to equalize all people. The article aroused incredulity and indignation in American liberals. As one reviewer commented: 'Miss Arendt's contempt for something she calls "the mob," her solicitude for "natural inequality," her concern for the values of diversity, led her (incredibly) to advance an argument that sanctions the liberty to deny constitutional liberties, the liberty of whites to deny constitutionl liberties to Negroes' (David Spitz, 'Politics and the Realm of Being,' 62).

74 *On Revolution*, 273
75 'Thoughts on Politics and Revolution: A Commentary,' Interview conducted by Adelbert Reif in the summer of 1970, in *Crises of the Republic*, 204
76 'Civil Disobedience,' in *Crises of the Republic*, 101
77 'Thoughts on Politics and Revolution,' 232–3
78 Morgenthau, 'Hannah Arendt on Totalitarianism and Democracy,' 129. In a similar vein, F.M. Barnard wrote of Arendt: 'She would like to suggest that somehow things need not get out of hand. Somehow political actions that are truly great *would* avoid brutality, words uttered in the public space *would not* be used to deceive; but she stipulates no moral restraints within the conception itself that would lend support to such assumptions' ('Infinity and Finality: Hannah Arendt on Politics and Truth,' 36).
79 Robert Nisbet, 'Hannah Arendt and the American Revolution,' 76
80 'The Crisis in Culture,' in *Between Past and Future*, 211
81 'Totalitarian Imperialism,' 43
82 I disagree with Bernard Crick when he says that for Arendt the great struggle was 'between the political or republican tradition and its totalitarian caricatures.' Crick wrote: 'If totalitarianism showed that "anything is possible," good government as common citizenship and social justice is still, to her, among those possibilities. This became more and more clear in her later writings' ('On Rereading *The Origins of Totalitarianism*,' 126). In fact, her later writings carry a pessimistic tone regarding such possibilities, as shall be shown in the final chapter of this book.
83 Whitfield, *Into the Dark*, 164
84 *On Revolution*, 138
85 Habermas, 'Hannah Arendt's Communications Concept of Power,' 15
86 As Habermas said: 'In systematically restricted communications, those involved form convictions subjectively free from restraint, convictions which are, however, illusionary. They thereby communicatively generate a power which, as soon as it is institutionalized, can also be used against them' (ibid., 22).
87 Wolin, 'Hannah Arendt: Democracy and the Political,' 18
88 Ibid., 14
89 Ibid., 18–19
90 Wolin, 'Hannah Arendt and the Ordinance of Time,' 96

91 'Hannah Arendt on Hannah Arendt,' in Melvyn Hill, ed., *The Recovery of the Public World*, 319–20
92 Ibid., 324
93 *Men in Dark Times*, ix
94 *Life of the Mind*, 1:4
95 Ibid., 1:5

Chapter 3: The Problem of Evil

1 *Eichmann in Jerusalem*, 8
2 Ibid., 269
3 Ibid., 272, 273
4 Ibid., 125–6
5 Ibid., 127–8
6 Lionel Abel interpreted Arendt's account as meaning the folliwng: 'If a man holds a gun at the head of another and forces him to kill his friend, the man with the gun will be aesthetically less ugly than the one who out of fear of death has killed his friend and perhaps did not even save his own life' ('The Aesthetics of Evil,' 219). This particular article received a response from Daniel Bell, who pointed out that Arendt's main concern in *Eichmann in Jerusalem* was justice, not aesthetics. Justice and aesthetics have something in common, in that in addressing them one must depart from the particular instance and question the universal 'principle' that guides particular actions. Bell concluded that 'it is this emphasis on justice which gives her judgments an abstract quality, a distancing which has been mistaken – cruelly, I believe – for an aesthetic judgment' ('The Alphabet of Justice,' 418).
7 Marie Syrkin, 'Hannah Arendt: The Clothes of the Empress,' 346. Other critics have suggested that in talking about the lack of resistance among victims of totalitarian rule, Arendt thereby inferred that the victims had behaved in ways unacceptable to her. Bernard Crick, for one, wrote: 'Her pagan, humanistic, existential ethics become quite clear: to be human is to act freely even if effective resistance is impossible. When prudence and compromise break down, or are impossible, compliance and hopeless resignation only feed the irrational belief of the new oppressors that some objective necessity, not man, rules' ('On Rereading *The Origins of Totalitarianism*,' 124).

I believe, with Daniel Bell, that such remarks show an insensitivity to the context of Arendt's writing. True, to be fully human, for her, was to be able to act freely, but the 'less than human' behaviour of all men under the strain of totalitarianism is *not* a responsibility shared equally by aggressors and victims. Arendt certainly never said that a man suffering internment and torture *ought* to resist his captors. In an answer to yet another critic, she expressed her confusion about the tendency among

her readers to accuse her of an indictment of Jews in Nazi Germany. The issue of
non-resistance had been raised by the prosecution at the trial, and as Arendt said: 'I
had reported this incident and dismissed the question twice as "silly and cruel
since it testified to a fatal ignorance of the conditions of the time"' ('The Formidable
Doctor Robinson: A Reply,' in *The Jew as Pariah* [1978], 260; originally published in the *New York Review of Books*, 20 Jan. 1966).

8 Gershom Scholem, '*Eichmann in Jerusalem*: An Exchange of Letters between
Gershom Scholem and Hannah Arendt,' in *The Jew as Pariah*, 240–5; originally
published in *Encounter Magazine*, 24 July 1963

9 *The Jew as Pariah*, 247 (Arendt's reply to Scholem's letter)

10 *Hannah Arendt: For Love of the World*, 354

11 *Eichmann in Jerusalem*, 286

12 Ibid., 288

13 Ibid., 277

14 Ibid., 294–5

15 Arendt explained that the cold-blooded criminal or the calculating liar is *less* of a
danger than the one who commits crimes out of thoughtlessness or ignorance,
because the former still understands that there is a difference between truth and
falsehood, between good and evil, whereas the latter does not. 'Arguments in
support of the statement "It is better to lie to others than to deceive yourself" would
have to point out that the cold-blooded liar remains aware of the distinction
between truth and falsehood, so the truth he is hiding from others has not yet been
manoeuvered out of the world altogether; it has found its last refuge in him
('Truth and Politics,' in *Between Past and Future*, 254–5).

16 Ibid., 259

17 Ibid., 264

18 *Human Condition*, 50

19 Ibid., 76–7

20 Ibid., 77

21 'On Humanity in Dark Times: Thoughts on Lessing,' in *Men in Dark Times*, 19

22 Ibid., 23

23 'What Is Existenz Philosophy? 46, note

24 *Hannah Arendt: For Love of the World*, 219

25 'Martin Heidegger at Eighty,' in Michael Murray, ed., *Heidegger and Modern
Philosophy* (New Haven and London: Yale University Press 1978), 303; originally
published in the *New York Review of Books* (October 1971)

26 Ibid., 303

27 Ibid., 299

28 Ibid., 303

29 Ibid., 299

30 *Nichomachean Ethics*, x, vii, 4–7
31 Iris Murdoch, *The Fire and the Sun*, 60
32 'Truth and Politics,' 245
33 Ibid., 247
34 *Life of the Mind*, 2:216
35 Ibid., 2:198
36 Ibid., 2:207
37 Ibid., 2:208
38 'The Conquest of Space and the Stature of Man,' in *Between Past and Future*, 279
39 Ibid., 280
40 'The Conquest of Space and the Stature of Man,' 275
41 'On Violence,' in *Crises of the Republic*, 108
42 Gray, 'The Winds of Thought,' 44
43 'Thinking and Moral Considerations,' 425
44 Ibid., 425–6
45 The association of thinking with death is explained more fully in *The Life of the Mind*. Arendt seemed, in this last book, to be fully accepting of the poetic links between thinking and dying, though she did not think the metaphor of death *the* definitive one for thinking. 'If we take our perspective from the world of appearances, the common world in which we appeared by birth and from which we shall disappear by death, then the wish to know our common habitat and amass all kinds of knowledge about it is natural. Because of thinking's need to transcend it, we have turned away; in a metaphorical sense, we have DISappeared from this world, and this can be understood – from the perspective of the natural and of our common-sense reasoning – as the anticipation of our final departure, that is, our death' (*Life of the Mind*, 1:83).
46 'Thinking and Moral Considerations,' 427
47 Ibid., 438
48 Ibid., 443
49 Ibid., 442
50 Ibid., 446
51 Ibid., 435
52 *Human Condition*, 324
53 *Life of the Mind*, 1:13

Chapter 4: The Life of the Mind

1 'Thinking and Moral Considerations,' 442
2 *Life of the Mind*, 1:11–12
3 Ibid., 1:52

4 Ibid., 1:5

5 Ricoeur, 'Action, Story and History,' 60–72

6 Ibid., 62

7 Ibid.

8 Arendt wrote that she had been plagued by certain doubts ever since completing *The Human Condition*. She had been concerned in that book with action, not thought, but as she said, 'the very term I adopted for my reflections on the matter, namely, *vita activa*, was coined by men who were devoted to the contemplative way of life, and who looked upon all kinds of being alive from that perspective' (*Life of the Mind*, 1:6).

9 Ibid., 1:45

10 Ibid., 1:45

11 Ibid., 1:213

12 Ibid., 1:213

13 Ibid., 1:210

14 Ibid., 1:76

15 Ibid., 1:78; emphasis mine

16 Ibid.

17 Arendt wrote emphatically, at the beginning of *The Life of the Mind*: 'In the world, which we enter, appearing from a nowhere and from which we disappear into a nowhere, *Being and Appearing coincide*' (*Life of the Mind*, 1:19).

18 Ibid., 1:52

19 Ibid., 1:200

20 To say that thinking beings have an urge to speak is different from saying that without discourse the need of reason could not be met. Arendt was of course aware that there are many accounts of reason that point beyond the limitations of the spoken word. The metaphor of sight is prevalent in the philosophic tradition where truth, or meaning, is understood as a vision and can only be partially rendered in speech. Plato was the first philosopher to suggest the 'possible incompatibility between intuition – the guiding metaphor for philosophic truth – and speech – the medium in which thinking manifests itself: the former always presents us with a contemporaneous manifold, whereas the latter necessarily discloses itself in a sequence of words and sentences. That the latter was a mere instrument for the former was axiomatic even for Plato, and remained axiomatic throughout the history of philosophy' (ibid., 1:118).

21 Ibid., 1:104

22 Ibid., 1:103

23 Ibid., 1:109

24 The text of the excerpt from Shakespeare's Richard III is cited by Arendt as follows:
What do I fear? Myself? There's none else by:

Richard loves Richard: that is, I am I.
Is there a murderer here? No, Yes, I am:
Then fly: what? from myself? Great reason why?
Lest I revenge. What! myself upon myself?
Alack! I love myself. Wherefore? For any good
That I myself have done unto myself?
O! no: alas! I rather hate myself
For hateful deeds committed by myself.
I am a villain. Yet I lie, I am not.
Fool, of thyself speak well: fool, do not flatter.
    (ibid., 1:189)

25 Ibid., 1:191
26 Ibid., 1:35
27 Ibid., 1:191, emphasis mine
28 Ibid., 1:205
29 Ibid., 1:210–11
30 Ibid., 1:213
31 Ibid., 2:14
32 Ibid., 2:38
33 Ibid., 2:27–8
34 Ibid., 2:19
35 Ibid., 2:42
36 Ibid., 2:47
37 Ibid., 2:170
38 Ibid., 2:168
39 Ibid., 2:21
40 Ibid., 2:194
41 Ibid., 2:193
42 Ibid., 2:208
43 Ibid., 2:211–12
44 Ibid., 2:216
45 Ibid., 2:95
46 I agree with Jean Yarborough and Peter Stern in their illuminating article on *The Life of the Mind*, when they write that, 'it may be that the evil in the world arises from our inclination toward nothingness, which would then account for its banality.' I would go further than the authors, however, in saying that the 'inclination toward nothingness' is an urge *specifically* attached to the faculty of the will (Yarborough and Stern, '*Vita Activa* and *Vita Contemplativa*,' 351).
47 *Origins of Totalitarianism*, 462
48 Ibid., 459

49 *Life of the Mind*, 2:103
50 Ibid., 1:219. Just after Arendt's death, the first page of 'Judging' was found in her typewriter, containing only the title and two epigraphs from Cicero and Goethe.
51 Ibid., 1:192
52 Ibid., 1:193
53 Ibid.
54 *Lectures on Kant's Political Philosophy*, 48
55 Ibid., 54
56 Ibid., 66
57 Ibid., 67
58 Ibid., 108
59 Ibid., 73
60 Ibid., 76
61 Ibid., 80
62 Ibid., 144
63 'The Crisis in Culture,' in *Between Past and Future*, 225
64 'Karl Jaspers: A Laudatio,' in *Men in Dark Times*, 79
65 'Isak Dinesen: 1885–1963,' in *Men in Dark Times*, 105
66 *Lectures on Kant's Political Philosophy*, Interpretive essay by Ronald Beiner, 143
67 Ibid., 153
68 *Life of the Mind*, 2:172
69 *Lectures on Kant's Political Philosophy*, Interpretive essay by Ronald Beiner, 153
70 Ibid., 153–4
71 *Life of the Mind*, 1:71
72 Ibid., 1:192
73 Clarke, 'Beyond "The Banality of Evil,"' 437
74 Ibid., 438
75 The image of the 'mental republic' is Elisabeth Young-Bruehl's: 'Hannah Arendt's *The Life of the Mind* is, to put the matter very simply, a treatise on mental good governance. Through a complexly woven series of reflections and analyses, Arendt tried to present an image of the three mental faculties checking and balancing each other like three branches of government.' Because Arendt did not live to complete her project, however, Young-Bruehl writes, 'the ideal – good governance, equality between the faculties – is clear, but a constitution for the mental republic was not drawn up' (*Hannah Arendt: For Love of the World*, 458).
76 'Karl Jaspers: A Laudatio,' in *Men in Dark Times*, 76
77 Barry Clarke has made the proper distinction, I think, between the freedom of the mental faculties and political freedom. It may well be, as he states, that 'true freedom, which distinguishes those who in times of crisis will draw the line and refuse to conform from those who will in all circumstances conform, … makes its

appearance only when values fundamental to the human condition are at stake' ('Beyond "The Banality of Evil,"' 435). This 'true freedom' becomes political by implication because it is so conspicuous. In a healthy community, it might appear ordinary and not very meaningful.

Also, I think Clarke is correct in maintaining that Arendt was not so hopeful as to think that the manifestations of critical thought in a few individuals could produce the seeds for political regeneration. The political effects of 'thinking' are neither direct, nor immediate. However, one can say that political regeneration is impossible *unless* people begin to think independently and critically. In this sense, as Clarke remarks, 'it is the choice to challenge rather than its political effectiveness that counts' ('Beyond "The Banality of Evil,"' 435).

78 Young-Bruehl, 'Reflection on Hannah Arendt's *The Life of the Mind*,' 303
79 'Hannah Arendt on Hannah Arendt,' in Melvyn Hill, ed., *The Recovery of The Public World*, 309

Chapter 5: *The* Vita Contemplativa *and Political Responsibility*

1 *Human Condition*, 9
2 Ibid., 7
3 Ibid., 140
4 Ibid., 160
5 Ibid., 177
6 Ibid., 118
7 Ibid., 8
8 Ibid., 123
9 Ibid., 22–3
10 *Lectures on Kant's Political Philosophy*, Interpretive essay by Ronald Beiner, 140
11 Habermas, 'Hannah Arendt's Communications Concept of Power,' 22
12 Ibid., 23
13 Ibid., 22
14 Beiner, *Political Judgment*, 27
15 Rosen, 'Thought and Action,' 65–84
16 'Hannah Arendt on Hannah Arendt,' in Melvyn Hill, ed., *The Recovery of the Public World*, 305
17 Rosen, 'Thought and Action,' 80
18 Gray, 'The Winds of Thought,' 59
19 Ibid., 60
20 'Karl Jaspers: A Laudatio,' 80
21 Jonas, *The Imperative of Responsibility*, 125
22 Ibid., 126

23 Ibid., 131
24 *Human Condition*, 247
25 'Karl Jaspers: A Laudatio,' 76
26 Ibid.
27 *Origins of Totalitarianism*, 466
28 'The Conquest of Space and the Stature of Man,' in *Between Past and Future*, 275–6
29 *Human Condition*, 322
30 Pitkin, 'Justice: On Relating Private and Public,' 339
31 Ibid., 347
32 Ibid., 348
33 'Personal Responsibility under Dictatorship,' broadcast over Pacifica Radio, 15 March 1964 (Boston, Mass.); cited in Elisabeth Young-Bruehl, *Hannah Arendt: For Love of the World*, 376
34 *Life of the Mind*, 1:167
35 Ibid., 1:190
36 Ibid., 190–1
37 *Nicomachean Ethics*, v, xi, 9–10
38 Ibid., v, i, 18
39 Ibid., v, vi, 4
40 *Life of the Mind*, 1:192
41 Ibid., 1:143
42 Ibid., 1:153
43 Ibid., 1:162
44 Ibid., 2:200. The separation between the 'We' and the 'I' in this passage (and elsewhere in Arendt's work for that matter) is marked largely by differing activities. In the plural, in political communities, we come together in order to create and change; in the singular (or between friends) we come together in order to strike harmony. In the plural, we will; in the singular, we reconcile. There is a sense of divided purpose implied here. Wilful action, change, and politics are contrasted with reflection, equilibrium, and friendship. Arendt's compartmentalization of mental activities remains troubling to some readers. Suzanne Jacobitti, for example, would like to produce out of Arendt's work a more integrated view of the self, one 'firmly in charge of all mental, psychic and bodily capacities,' one with 'integration of character, reason and desire' ('Hannah Arendt and the Will,' 65). B. Honig responds to Jacobitti by saying that Arendt's view of the 'self' is simply not integrated in the way that Jacobitti would like, and that Arendt would have rejected any such understanding. Arendt did not want to create 'a self in charge of itself,' to the extent that this certainty of self would preclude the possibilities of new beginnings in the world. The will, the 'spring of action' as Arendt defined it, is critical to Arendt's view of freedom and plurality. In Jacobitti's revision of

Arendt 'the self is made stronger,' but 'the contingency of the human world, so valued by Arendt, is diminished, and so are the possibilities for the introduction of novelty into the world' ('Arendt, Identity and Difference,' 89).

45 *Nicomachean Ethics*, VIII, i, 4
46 Ibid., VIII, vii, 4
47 *Life of the Mind*, 1:167
48 Ibid., 1:168
49 'Lessing: On Humanity in Dark Times,' in *Men in Dark Times*, 22
50 Clarke, 'Beyond "The Banality of Evil,"' 435
51 *Between Past and Future*, 4
52 *Men in Dark Times*, ix
53 *On Revolution*, 181
54 *Life of the Mind*, 2:201–2
55 *Human Condition*, 5
56 She once remarked: 'Everything which really can be figured out, in the sphere Engels called the administration of things – these are social things in general. That they should then be subject to debate seems to me phony and a plague' ('On Hannah Arendt,' in Melvyn Hill, ed., *The Recovery of the Public World*, 317).
57 Ibid., 323
58 *Human Condition*, 135
59 Spoken at the funeral service for Hannah Arendt, at the Riverside Memorial Chapel in New York City, Monday, 8 December 1975
60 Vollrath, 'Hannah Arendt and the Method of Political Thinking,' 182

Bibliography

Hannah Arendt

Comprehensive bibliographies of Arendt's work can be found in Elisabeth Young-Bruehl, *Hannah Arendt: For Love of the World* (New Haven: Yale University Press 1982), 535–47; and Melvyn Hill, ed., *Hannah Arendt: The Recovery of the Public World* (New York: St Martin's Press 1979), 342–54.

Books

1951 *The Origins of Totalitarianism.* New York: Harcourt, Brace and Co. 2d enl. ed. New York: Meridian Books 1958. 3d ed., with new prefaces, New York: Harcourt, Brace and World 1966, 1968, 1973

1958 *The Human Condition.* Chicago: University of Chicago Press. Repr. New York: Doubleday Anchor 1959

1958 *Rachel Varnhagen: The Life of a Jewish Woman.* Original English ed. London: East and West Library. Repr. New York: Harcourt, Brace, Jovanovich 1974

1961 *Between Past and Future: Six Exercises in Political Thought.* New York: Viking. Rev. ed. 1968

1963 Eichmann in Jerusalem: A Report on the Banality of Evil. New York: Viking. Rev. ed. 1965

1963 *On Revolution.* New York: Viking. Rev. ed. 1965

1968 *Men in Dark Times.* New York: Harcourt, Brace and World

1970 *On Violence.* New York: Harcourt, Brace and World

1972 *Crises of the Republic.* New York: Harcourt, Brace, Jovanovich

1978 *The Jew as Pariah: Jewish Identity and Politics in the Modern Age.* Edited by Ron H. Feldman. New York: Grove

1978 *The Life of the Mind.* 2 vols. Edited by Mary McCarthy. New York: Harcourt, Brace, Jovanovich

1982 *Lectures on Kant's Political Philosophy*. Edited by Ronald Beiner. Chicago: University of Chicago Press

Articles

1944 'The Jew as Pariah: A Hidden Tradition.' *Jewish Social Studies* 6/2 (February): 99–122
1945 'Approaches to the "German Problem."' *Partisan Review* 12/1 (Winter): 93–106
1945 'Organized Guilt and Universal Responsibility.' *Jewish Frontier* (January): 19–23
1946 'French Existentialism.' *Nation* 23 (February): 226–8
1946 'Imperialism: Road to Suicide.' *Commentary* 1 (February): 27–35
1946 'What Is Existenz Philosophy?' *Partisan Review* 8/1 (Winter): 34–56
1949 'Totalitarian Terror.' *Review of Politics* 11/1 (January): 112–15
1950 'The Aftermath of Nazi Rule, Report from Germany.' *Commentary* 10 (October): 342–53
1950 'Religion and the Intellectuals, a Symposium.' *Partisan Review* 17 (February): 113–16
1953 'Reply to Eric Voegelin's Review of *The Origins of Totalitarianism*.' *Review of Politics* 15 (January): 76–85
1953 'Religion and Politics.' *Confluence* 2/3 (September): 105–26
1953 'Understanding and Politics.' *Partisan Review* 20/4 (August): 377–92
1953 'Understanding Communism.' *Partisan Review* 20/5 (October): 580–3
1956 'Authority in the Twentieth Century.' *Review of Politics* 18/4 (October): 403–17
1957 'History and Immortality.' *Partisan Review* 24/1 (Winter): 11–53
1958 'Totalitarian Imperialism: Reflections on the Hungarian Revolution.' *Journal of Politics* 20/1 (February): 5–43
1959 'Reflections on Little Rock.' *Dissent* 6/1 (Winter): 45–56
1962 'Action and "The Pursuit of Happiness."' In *Politische Ordnung und Menschliche Existenz: Festgabe für Eric Voegelin*. Munich: Beck
1962 'The Cold War and the West.' *Partisan Review* 29/1 (Winter): 10–20
1963 'Man's Conquest of Space.' *American Scholar* 32 (Autumn): 527–40
1964 'Personal Responsibility under Dictatorship.' *Listener* (6 August): 185–7, 205
1966 'The Formidable Dr. Robinson: A Reply to the Jewish Establishment.' *New York Review of Books* 5/12 (20 January): 26–30
1966 Introduction to *The Warriors* by J. Glenn Gray. New York: Harper and Row
1967 Preface to *The Future of Germany* by Karl Jaspers. Chicago: University of Chicago Press
1968 'He's All Dwight: Dwight Macdonald's *Politics*.' *New York Review of Books* 11/2 (1 August): 31–3
1971 'Martin Heidegger at Eighty.' *New York Review of Books* 17/6 (21 October): 50–4
1971 'Thinking and Moral Considerations.' *Social Research* 38/3 (Fall): 417–46
1975 'Remembering Wystan H. Auden.' *New Yorker* (20 January): 39–40

1975 'Home to Roost.' *New York Review of Books* (26 June): 3–6
1977 'Public Rights and Private Interests.' In *Small Comforts for Hard Times: Humanists on Public Policy*. Edited by Mooney and Stuber. New York: Columbia University Press
1978 'From an Interview.' *New York Review of Books* 25/16 (26 October): 18

Secondary Sources

Books

Aristotle. *Nichomachean Ethics*. Trans. by H. Rackham. Cambridge, Mass., and London: Loeb Classical Library 1926
Ball, Terrence, ed. *Political Theory and Praxis: New Perspectives*. Minneapolis: University of Minnesota Press 1977
Beiner, Ronald. *Political Judgment*. Chicago: The University of Chicago Press 1983
Bernstein, Richard J. *Beyond Objectivism and Relativism: Science, Hermeneutics, and Praxis*. Philadelphia: University of Pennsylvania Press 1983
Boyers, Robert, ed. *Proceedings of History, Ethics, Politics: A Conference Based on the Work of Hannah Arendt*. Saratoga Springs, NY: Empire College 1982
Buchheim, Hans. *Totalitarian Rule: Its Nature and Characteristics*. Translated by Ruth Hein. Middletown, Conn.: Wesleyan University Press 1968
Canovan, Margaret. *The Political Thought of Hannah Arendt*. London: J.M. Dent and Sons 1974
Crick, Bernard. *In Defence of Politics*. Baltimore: Penguin 1964
Friedrich, Carl, ed. *Totalitarianism*. Cambridge: Harvard University Press 1954
Friedrich, Carl, and Zbigniew Brzezinski. *Totalitarian Dictatorship and Autocracy*. Cambridge: Harvard University Press 1956, 1965
Gray, J. Glenn. *The Warriors: Reflections on Men in Battle*. New York: Harper Colophon Books 1959, 1970
Hill, Melvyn A., ed. *Hannah Arendt: The Recovery of the Public World*. New York: St Martin's Press 1979
Hughes, H. Stuart. *The Sea Change: The Migrations of Social Thought, 1930–1965*. New York: Harper and Row 1975
Jonas, Hans. *The Phenomenon of Life: Toward a Philosophical Biology*. Chicago: University of Chicago Press 1966
– *Philosophical Essays: From Ancient Creed to Technological Man*. Chicago: University of Chicago Press 1974
– *The Imperative of Responsibility*. Chicago: University of Chicago Press 1984
Kateb, George. *Hannah Arendt: Politics, Conscience, Evil*. Totowa, NJ: Rowman and Allanheld 1983
Menze, Ernest, ed. *Totalitarianism Reconsidered*. New York: Kennikat 1981

Moehle, N.R. *The Dimensions of Evil and Transcendence*. Washington: University Press of America 1978

Murdoch, Iris. *The Fire and the Sun: Why Plato Banned the Artists*. New York: Oxford University Press 1977

Neumann, Sigmund. *Permanent Revolution*. New York: Praeger 1965

Niemeyer, Gerhart. *Between Nothingness and Paradise*. Baton Rouge: Louisiana State University Press 1971

Parekh, Bikhu. *Hannah Arendt and the Search for a New Political Philosophy*. London and Basingstoke: Macmillan Press 1981

Plato. *The Republic*. Trans. Allan Bloom. New York: Basic Books 1968

Polin, Claude. *Le Totalitarisme*. Paris: Presses Universitaires de France 1982

Riley, Patrick. *Will and Political Legitimacy: A Critical Exposition of Social Contract Theory in Hobbes, Locke, Rousseau, Kant, and Hegel*. Cambridge: Harvard University Press 1982

Sennett, Richard. *The Fall of Public Man*. London: Cambridge University Press 1977

Solzhenitsyn, Alexander. *The Gulag Archipelago*. 3 vols. New York: Harper and Row 1978

Strauss, Leo, ed. *On Tyranny*. New York: Cornell University Press 1968

Talmon, J.L. *The Origins of Totalitarian Democracy*. New York: Praeger 1970

Tolle, Gordon. *Human Nature under Fire*. Washington, DC: University Press of America 1982

Tucker, Robert C., ed. *The Great Purge Trial*. New York: Grosset and Dunlap 1965

Whitfield, Stephen J. *Into the Dark: Hannah Arendt and Totalitarianism*. Philadelphia: Temple University Press 1980

Young-Bruehl, Elisabeth. *Hannah Arendt: For Love of the World*. New Haven: Yale University Press 1982

Articles

Abel, Lionel. 'The Aesthetics of Evil.' *Partisan Review* 30/2 (Summer 1963): 211–30

Adamson, W. 'Beyond Reform and Revolution: Notes on Political Education in Gramsci, Habermas and Arendt.' *Theory and Society* 6/3 (November 1978): 429–60

Alvarez, A. 'The State of Man.' *New Statesman* 57/7 (March 1959): 336–7

Bakan, Mildred. 'Hannah Arendt's Concepts of Labour and Work.' In Melvyn Hill, ed., *The Recovery of the Public World*, 49–66

Barnard, F. Mencher. 'Infinity and Finality: Hannah Arendt on Politics and Truth.' *Canadian Journal of Political and Social Theory* 1/3 (Fall 1977): 29–57

Baron, S.W. 'Personal Notes: Hannah Arendt.' *Jewish Social Studies* 38/2 (Spring 1976): 187-9

Beatty, J. 'Thinking and Moral Considerations: Socrates' and Arendt's Eichmann.' *Journal of Value Inquiry* 10 (Winter 1976)

Beiner, Ronald. 'Judging in a World of Apearances: A Commentary on Hannah Arendt's Unwritten Finale.' *History of Political Thought* 1/1 (Spring 1980): 117–35
– 'Hannah Arendt's Kant Lectures.' Paper presented at the New School for Social Research, 5 November 1982
– Interpretive essay 'Hannah Arendt on Judging.' In R. Beiner, ed., Hannah Arendt, *Lectures on Kant's Political Philosophy*, 89–156. Chicago: University of Chicago Press 1982
Bell, Daniel. 'The Alphabet of Justice: Reflections on *Eichmann in Jerusalem.*' *Partisan Review* 30/3 (Fall 1963): 417–29
Bennett, John. Review of *The Human Condition* in *American Anthropologist* 69 (August 1959): 684–8
Bernstein, Richard J. 'Hannah Arendt: The Ambiguities of Theory and Practice.' In Terrence Ball, ed., *Political Theory and Praxis*, 144–58
– 'Hannah Arendt: Judging – the Actor and the Spectator' In Robert Boyers, ed., *Proceedings of History, Ethics, Politics*
Botstein, Leon. 'Liberating the Pariah: Politics, the Jews, and Hannah Arendt.' *Salmagundi* 60 (Summer 1983): 73–106
Boulding, Kenneth. 'Philosophy, Behavioural Science and the Nature of Man.' *World Politics* 12/2 (January 1960): 272–9
Burrowes, Robert. Review of *The Origins of Totalitarianism* in *World Politics* 21/2 (January 1969): 272–94
Canovan, Margaret. 'The Contradictions of Arendt's Political Thought.' *Political Theory* 6/1 (February 1978): 5–26
– 'A Case of Distorted Communication: A Note on Habermas and Arendt.' *Political Theory* 11/1 (February 1983): 105–16
– 'Pilkin, Arendt, and Justice.' *Political Theory* 10/3 (August 1982)
Castoriadis, Cornelius. 'The Destinies of Totalitarianism.' *Salmagundi* 60 (Summer 1983): 107–22
Clarke, Barry. 'Beyond "The Banality of Evil."' *British Journal of Political Science* 10 (1980): 417–39
Cooper, Leroy. 'Hannah Arendt's Political Philosophy: An Interpretation.' *Review of Politics* 38/2 (April 1976): 145–76
Crick, Bernard. 'On Rereading *The Origins of Totalitarianism.*' *Social Research* 44/1 (Spring 1977): 106–26
Denneny, Michael. 'The Privilege of Ourselves: Hannah Arendt on Judgment.' In Melvyn Hill, ed., *The Recovery of the Public World*, 245–74
Donague, D. 'After Reading Hannah Arendt.' *Poetry* 100/2 (May 1962): 127–30
Dossa, Shiraz. 'Human Status and Politics: Hannah Arendt on the Holocaust.' *Canadian Journal of Political Science* 13/2 (June 1980): 309–23

Draenos, Stan Spyros. 'Thinking without a Ground: Hannah Arendt and the Contemporary Situation of Understanding.' In Melvyn Hill, ed., *The Recovery of the Public World*, 209–24

– 'The Totalitarian Theme in the Work of Max Horkheimer and Hannah Arendt.' Paper presented at the State University of New York, Albany, 6 February 1980

Elevitch, Bernard. 'Arendt and Heidegger: The Illusion of Politics.' *Boston University Journal* 20 (1972)

Forester, John. 'Hannah Arendt and Critical Theory: A Critical Response.' *Journal of Politics* 43 (February 1981): 196–202

Frampton, Kenneth. 'The Status of Man and the Status of His Objects: A Reading of *The Human Condition*.' In Melvyn Hill, ed., *The Recovery of the Public World*, 101–30

Frankel, Charles. Review of *The Human Condition* in *Political Science Quarterly* 74 (Summer 1959): 420–2

Frimstad, John. 'The Irrelevance of the Inevitable.' *Journal of Politics* 37/2 (May 1975): 362–92

Fruchter, Norman. 'Arendt's Eichmann and Jewish Identity.' In J. Weinstein and D. Eakins, eds, *For a New America*, 423–54. New York: Vintage 1970

Fuss, Peter. 'Hannah Arendt's Conception of Political Community.' *Idealist Studies* 3/3 (September 1973)

Glazer, Nathan. 'Hannah Arendt's America.' *Commentary* 60/3 (September 1975): 61–7

Gray, J. Glenn. 'The Winds of Thought.' *Social Research* 44/1 (Spring 1977): 44–62

– 'Meditations on the Intimate and the Ultimate: Excerpts from the Philosophical Journals of J. Glenn Gray.' *Philosophy Today* (Summer 1981): 114–17

Gray, Sherry. 'Hannah Arendt and the Solitariness of Thinking.' *Philosophy Today* xxv, 2/4 (Summer 1981): 121–30

Gross, John. 'Arendt on Eichmann.' *Encounter* 21/5 (November 1963): 65–74

Habermas, Jürgen. 'Hannah Arendt's Concept of Power.' *Merkur* 30/10 (October 1976): 946–60

– 'Hannah Arendt's Communications Concept of Power.' *Social Research* 44/1 (Spring 1977): 3–23

Heather, Gerard P., and Matthew Stolz. 'Hannah Arendt and the Problem of Critical Theory.' *Journal of Politics* 41 (February 1979): 1–22

Heller, Erich. 'Hannah Arendt as a Critic of Literature.' *Social Research* 44/1 (Spring 1977): 147–59

Hill, Melvyn A. 'The Fictions of Mankind and the Stories of Men.' In Melvyn Hill, ed., *The Recovery of the Public World*, 275–300

Hinchman, Sandra. 'Common Sense and Political Barbarism in the Theory of Hannah Arendt.' *Polity* 17/2 (1984): 317–39

Honeywell, J.A. 'Revolution: Its Potentialities and Its Degradations.' *Ethics* 80/4 (July 1970): 251–65

Honig, B. 'Arendt, Identity and Difference,' *Political Theory* 6/2 (February 1988): 77–98

Howe, Irving. '*The New Yorker* and Hannah Arendt.' *Commentary* 36 (October 1963): 318–19

Jacobitti, Suzanne. 'Hannah Arendt and the Will.' *Political Theory* 6/1 (February 1988): 53–75

Jacobson, Norman. 'Parable and Paradox: In Response to Arendt's *On Revolution.*' *Salmagundi* 60 (Summer 1983): 123–39

Jay, Martin. 'Hannah Arendt: Opposing Views.' *Partisan Review* 45/3 (1978): 348–80

Jonas, Hans. Words spoken at the funeral service for Hannah Arendt, New York City, 8 December 1975

– 'Hannah Arendt as a Philosopher.' Paper delivered at the Hannah Arendt Memorial Symposium, New School for Social Research, 23 April 1976

– 'Acting, Knowing, Thinking: Gleanings from Hannah Arendt's Philosophical Work.' *Social Research* 44/1 (Spring 1977): 25–43

Justman, Stewart. 'Hannah Arendt and the Idea of Disclosure.' *Philosophy and Social Criticism* 4/8 (1981): 407–23

Kateb, George. 'Freedom and Worldliness in the Thought of Hannah Arendt.' *Political Theory* 5/2 (1977): 141–82

– 'Arendt and Representative Democracy.' *Salmagundi* 60 (Summer 1983): 20–59

– 'Death and Politics: Hannah Arendt's Reflections on the American Constitution.' *Social Research* 54/3 (Autumn 1987): 605–28

Krauer, James T. 'Motives and Goals in Hannah Arendt's Concept of Political Action.' *American Political Science Review* 74 (September 1980): 721–33

Lasch, Christopher. 'Introduction.' *Salmagundi* 60 (Summer 1983): iv–xvi

Levin, Martin. 'On *Animal Laborans* and *Homo Politicus.*' *Political Theory* 7/4 (November 1979): 521–31

Luban, D. 'On Habermas, on Arendt, on Power.' *Philosophy and Social Criticism* 6 (Spring 1979): 79–95

– 'Explaining Dark Times: Hannah Arendt's Theory of Theory,' *Social Research* (Summer 1983): 215–47

Major, Robert W. 'A Reading of Hannah Arendt's "Unusual" Distinction between Labour and Work.' In Melvyn Hill, ed., *The Recovery of the Public World*, 131–56

May, W. '*Animal Laborans* and *Homo Faber*: Reflections on a Theology of Work.' *Thomist* 36 (October 1972)

McCarthy, Mary. Review of *The Human Condition* in *New Yorker*, 18 October 1958

McKenna, G. 'On Hannah Arendt: Politics As It Is, Was, Might Be.' *Salmagundi* 10–11 (Fall 1969–Spring 1970): 104–22

Miller, James. 'The Pathos of Novelty: Hannah Arendt's Image of Freedom in the Modern World.' In Melvyn Hill, ed., *The Recovery of The Public World*, 177–208

Moors, Kent F. 'The Structure of Hannah Arendt's *Life of the Mind.*' *Political Science Reviewer* 10 (1980): 189–230

Morgenthau, Hans J. 'Hannah Arendt (1906–1975): An Appreciation.' *Political Theory* 4/1 (February 1976): 5–8
– 'Hannah Arendt on Totalitarianism and Democracy.' *Social Research* 44/1 (Spring 1977): 127–31
Nelson, John S. 'Politics and Truth: Arendt's Problematic.' *American Journal of Political Science* 22 (1978): 270–301
Nisbet, Robert. 'Hannah Arendt and the American Revolution.' *Social Research* 44/1 (Spring 1977): 63–79
Oakeshott, Michael. Review of *Between Past and Future* in *Political Science Quarterly* 77 (March 1962): 88–90
Okin, Susan M. 'Hannah Arendt and the Realm of Necessity.' Paper presented at the American Political Science Association meetings, San Francisco, September 1975
O'Sullivan, N.K. 'Politics, Totalitarianism and Freedom: The Political Thought of Hannah Arendt.' *Political Studies* 21/2 (June 1973): 183–98
– 'Hannah Arendt: Hellenic Nostalgia and Industrial Society.' In A. de Crespigny and K. Minogue, eds., *Contemporary Political Philosophers*, 228–51. New York: Dodds, Mead 1975
Parekh, Bikhu. 'Hannah Arendt's Critique of Marx.' In Melvyn Hill, ed., *The Recovery of the Public World*, 67–100
Pitkin, Hanna Fenichel. 'The Roots of Conservatism: Michael Oakeshott and the Denial of Politics.' *Dissent* (Fall 1973): 496–526
– 'Justice: On Relating Private and Public.' *Political Theory* 9/3 (August 1981): 327–52
Ricoeur, Paul. 'Action, Story and History: On Re-reading *The Human Condition*.' *Salmagundi* (Summer 1983): 60–72
Riley, Patrick, 'Hannah Arendt on Kant, Truth and Politics.' *Political Studies* 35 (1987): 379–92
Rosen, Stanley. 'Thought and Action.' *Inquiry* 2 (1959): 65–84
Rubinoff, L. 'The Dialectic of Work and Labour in the Ontology of Man.' *Humanitas* 7 (Fall 1971)
Schwartz, Benjamin I. 'The Religion of Politics.' *Dissent* (April 1970): 144–62
Shklar, Judith N. Review of *Between Past and Future* in *History and Theory* 2 (1962): 286–92
– 'Hannah Arendt's Triumph.' *New Republic* 27 (December 1975): 8–10
– 'Rethinking the Past.' *Social Research* 44/1 (Spring 1977): 80–90
– 'Hannah Arendt as Pariah.' *Partisan Review* (1983), no. 1, 64–77
Spitz, David. 'Politics and the Realm of Being.' *Dissent* 6 (1959): 56–65
Sternbergen, Dolf. 'The Sunken City: Hannah Arendt's Idea of Politics.' *Social Research* 44/1 (Spring 1977): 132–46
Stillman, P.G. 'Freedom as Participation: The Revolutionary Theory of Hegel and Arendt.' *American Behavioural Scientist* 20/4 (April 1977): 477–92

Suchting, W.A. 'Marx and Hannah Arendt's *Human Condition.*' *Ethics* 73 (1962/63): 47–55

Syrkin, Marie. 'Hannah Arendt: The Clothes of the Empress.' *Dissent* 10/4 (Autumn 1963): 344–52

Voegelin, Eric. Review of *The Origins of Totalitarianism* in *Review of Politics* 15 (January 1953): 68–85

Vollrath, Ernst. 'Hannah Arendt and the Method of Political Thinking.' *Social Research* 44/1 (Spring 1977): 160–82

Wieseltier, Leon. 'Understanding Anti-Semitism: Hannah Arendt on the Origins of Prejudice.' *New Republic* 482–3 (October 7–14, 1981): 29–32 and 29–34

Wolin, Sheldon S. 'Hannah Arendt and the Ordinance of Time.' *Social Research* 44/1 (Spring 1977): 91–105

– 'Stopping to Think.' *New York Review of Books*, 26 October 1978

– 'Hannah Arendt: Democracy and the Political.' *Salmagundi* 60 (Summer 1983): 3–19

Yarbrough, Jean, and Peter Stern. 'Hannah Arendt.' *The American Scholar* 47 (Summer 1978)

– '*Vita Activa* and *Vita Contemplativa*: Reflections on Hannah Arendt's Political Thought in *The Life of the Mind.*' *Review of Politics* (July 1981): 323–54

Young-Bruehl, Elisabeth. 'Hannah Arendt's Storytelling.' *Social Research* 44/1 (Spring 1977): 183–90

– 'From the Pariah's Point of View: Reflections on Hannah Arendt's Life and Work.' In Melvyn Hill, ed., *The Recovery of the Public World*, 3–26

– 'Reflections on Hannah Arendt's *The Life of the Mind.*' *Political Theory* 10/2 (May 1982): 277–305

Index

Abel, Lionel, 139n6
Achilles, 31
action, 10, 16, 36, 72, 100; intelligibility
  of, 107; revolutionary, 103
Alvarez, A., 23
American founding, 88
animal laborans, 14–15, 17–20, 22, 25,
  28–9, 45, 57, 101
Aristotle, 4, 24, 26, 117, 122
art, 19
Augustine, St, 15; love in, 90; on the will,
  90
authority, 46

Bakan, Mildred, 24–6
Bay, Christian, 99
Beiner, Ronald, 95–7, 104, 106
Bell, Daniel, 139n6
Bennett, John, 21
Bergson, Henri, 20
Bolsheviks, 47
Brzezinski, Zbigniew, 40
Buchheim, Hans, 42

Camus, Albert, 33
Canovan, Margaret, 21–3
Cato, 19, 103
Christianity, 16, 135n25

citizenship, 120
civil rights, American, 56
Clarke, Barry, 97–8, 121; on the will,
  144n77
class, 60, 131n68
common sense, 35–6, 44, 78, 128n24;
  relation to taste, 93; and worldliness,
  93
concentration camps, 48
conscience, 74–5, 116
consciousness, 77
Crick, Bernard, 138n82
crime, 140n15; totalitarian, 63
culture, 57

Darwin, Charles, 47
death, 32–3, 73; and thinking, 141n45
democracy, 49, 51; council, 54–5; liberal,
  48
Descartes, René, 26–8, 81
desegregation, 137n73
Dinesen, Isak, 95
Duns Scotus, 86

Eichmann, Adolf, 7, 37, 61, 63, 103, 114;
  and willing, 97–8
empiricism, 21
Epictetus, 86

metaphysical fallacies, 127n6
miracle, 46, 111–12
Montesquieu, Baron de, 122
moral concepts, 134n4
Morgenthau, Hans, 56
mortality, 29, 33

natality, 11, 29, 52, 111, 113, 131n74
Nazis, 47, 63
Nietzsche, Friedrich, 20, 27, 86; and
    eternal return, 88, 96, 109; and the will,
    87
nihilism, 75

Parmenides, 94
Paul, St, 86
phenomenology, 21
Pitkin, Hannah, 114, 121
Plato, 15–16, 20, 26, 30–1, 33, 46, 71,
    73–4, 80–1, 135n25, 142n20;
    cave allegory, 127n4; and eternity,
    132n79; relation to Heidegger, 70;
    Republic, 4
plurality, 3, 7, 20, 23, 41, 101–2, 109,
    120, 127n1; and revolution, 53
power, 48, 137n53; definition of, 121
private, 11; happiness, 55; realm, 12, 114;
    life, 121
progress, 86
propaganda, 45
property, 123
psychoanalysis, 134n5
psychology, 83
public, 11; happiness, 54; participation, 23;
    realm, 12, 49, 114–15; space, 19,
    50–2, 71

reification, 13
republic of faculties, 98, 144n75
Resistance, 121

revolution, 52; American, 53; and freedom,
    57; French, 52; Hungarian, 51, 55,
    130n48
Ricoeur, Paul, 78–9
Roman founding, 47, 88
Rosen, Stanley, 107–8

scepticism, 115
Scholem, Gershom, 65
Schopenhauer, Arthur, 80
science, 19, 28–9, 31, 72, 103, 112,
    129n34
sense perception, 80
Shakespeare, William, 82, 116; *Richard III*,
    142n24
society, 12, 15, 53; American, 56
Socrates, 71, 74, 108, 110, 117–18, 120;
    Republic, 116
Solzhenitsyn, Alexander, 43
soul, 108
Soviet council system, 22
spectator, 92
Stalin, Joseph, 39
Strauss, Leo, 5, 135n11
Strawson, P.F., 79
Syrkin, Marie, 139n7

taste, 92–3; relation to judging, 94
temporality, 83, 111; and Hegel,
    87
terror, 41, 43, 48–50, 53, 112
thinking: definition of, 78; and death, 80;
    and morality, 84; and political conse-
    quences, 99; and responsibility, 111; and
    transcendence, 83; and tragedy, 84; as
    two-in-one, 82; as withdrawal, 80–1,
    118
Tocqueville, Alexis de, 51
Tucker, Robert, 136n34
tyranny, 42, 61, 135n11